W9-CNH-440

◈ UNIVERSAL MYTHS ◈

END OF DAYS

DOOMSDAY MYTHS AROUND THE WORLD

BY BLAKE HOENA

ILLUSTRATED BY FELIPE KROLL

CAPSTONE PRESS
a capstone imprint

Graphic Library is published by Capstone Press,
1710 Roe Crest Drive, North Mankato, Minnesota 56003
www.mycapstone.com

Library of Congress Cataloging-in-Publication data is available on the Library of Congress website.
ISBN 978-1-5157-6626-1 (library binding)
ISBN 978-1-5157-6630-8 (paperback)
ISBN 978-1-5157-6634-6 (eBook PDF)

Summary: Read tales of devastating destruction in eight doomsday myths from various mythologies and
traditions around the world — all told in gripping graphic novel format.

Editor
Abby Huff

Art Director
Nathan Gassman

Designer
Ted Williams

Media Researcher
Jo Miller

Production Specialist
Kathy McColley

Cover Illustrator
Greg Taylor

Thanks to our consultant, Daniel Peretti, PhD, for lending his expertise and advice.

Design Element: Shutterstock: dalmingo (map),
ilolab, maradon 333, Milos Djapovic, NuConcept Dezine

Printed and bound in the United States of America.
092017 010743R

TABLE OF CONTENTS

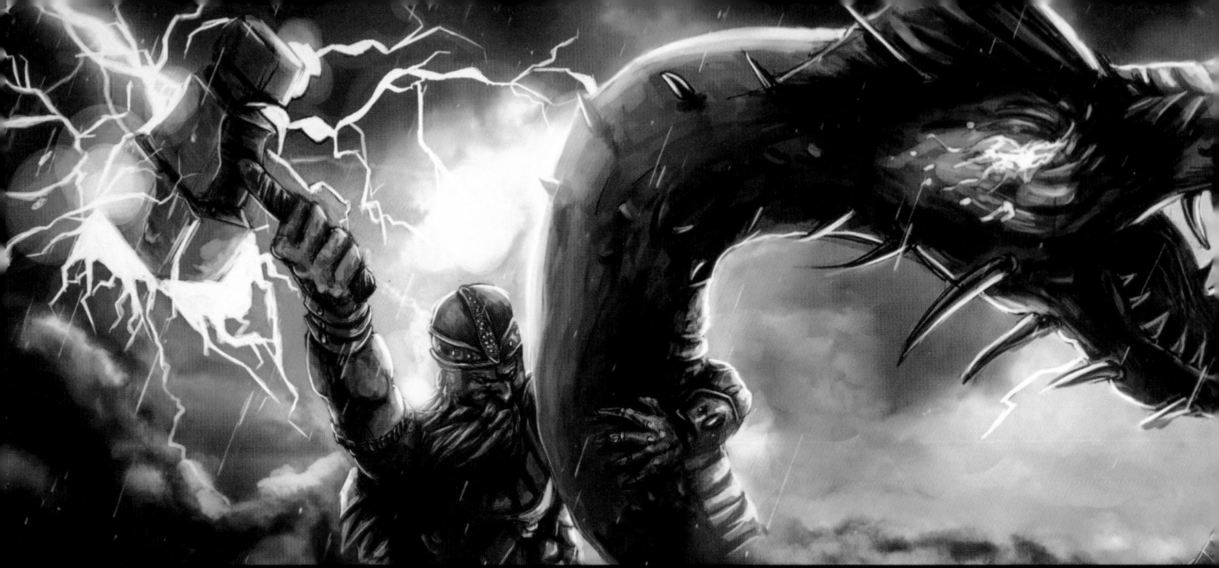

FLOODS, FIRE, AND BLOOD

The end of the world is near! A raging fire sweeps across the land, reducing all life to ash. Waters swell and wash over everything in a terrible flood. The whole world shakes and trembles, crumbling into nothingness. Mighty gods face off in a fierce cosmic war that lays waste to all. In myths of old, events such as these were foretold to bring an end to life on Earth.

Every culture, from ancient Norse to Native American, has its own myths and legends. Myths played an important role in the lives of ancient peoples. Long ago, people did not have the sciences to explain why lightning flashed and thunder boomed. They did not know what caused earthquakes or floods. Instead, they told stories, or myths, to help them make sense of life.

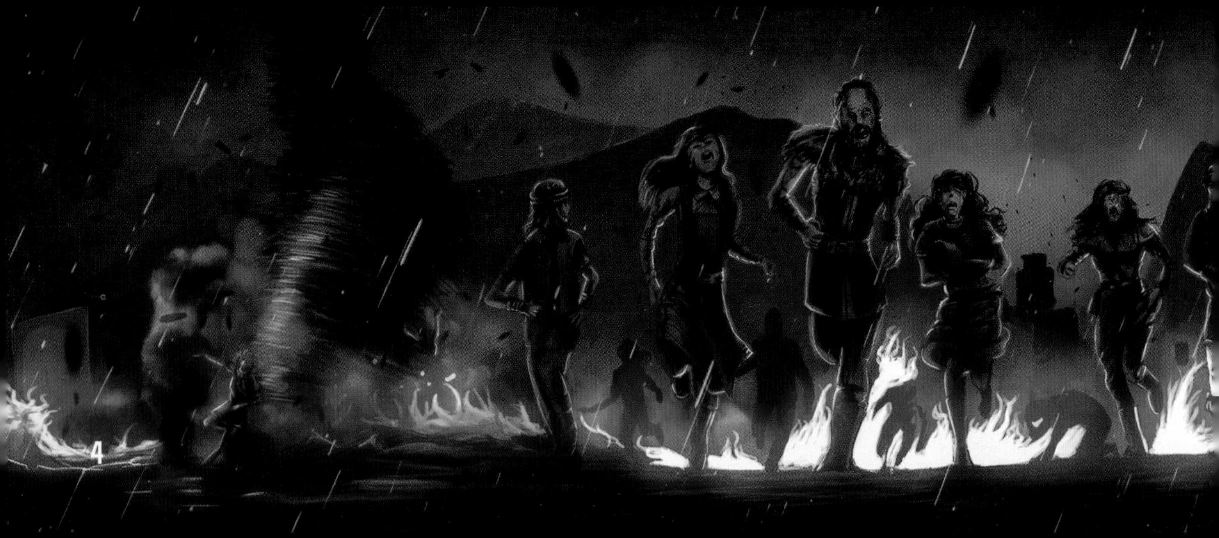

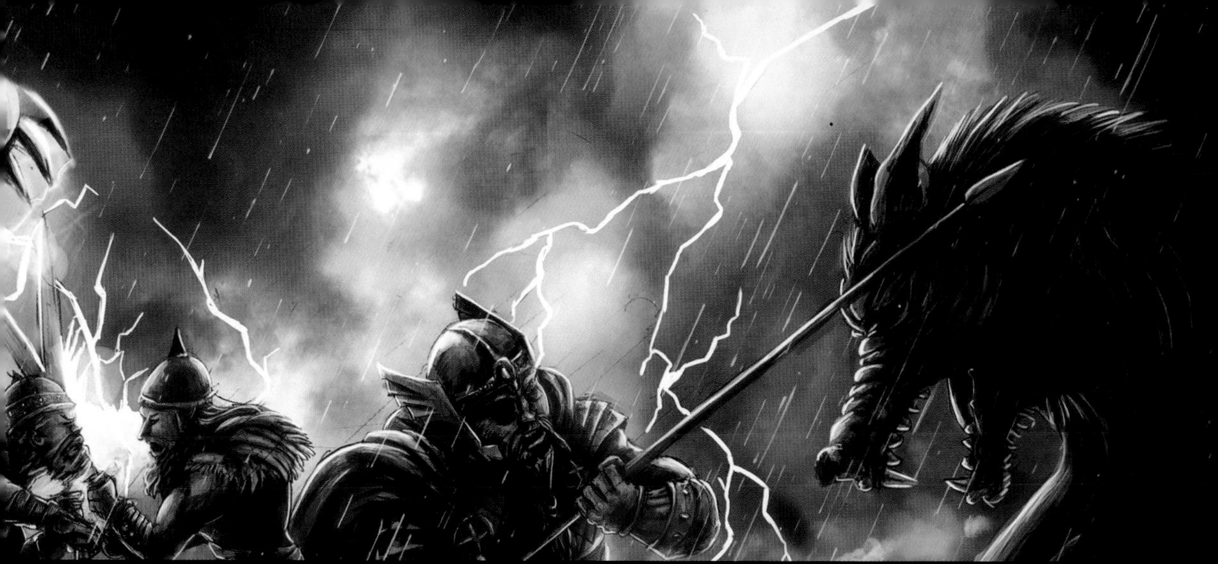

Cultures from around the world often share similar myths, including stories of devastating destruction. The end may come as a flood, earthquake, or as the result of a cataclysmic battle between the gods. But in most mythologies, the world does not end forever. Rather, doomsday myths often tell about the end of an age or era. Old civilizations give way to the creation of a new age. Sometimes several worlds have existed and been destroyed before the one in which we live now was created.

In many cases, life was wiped out because it was imperfect. People had grown corrupt and did not respect the gods. The following tales served as warnings to ancient peoples — behave well and honor the gods, or else. If they didn't, the powerful deities could bring an end to everything.

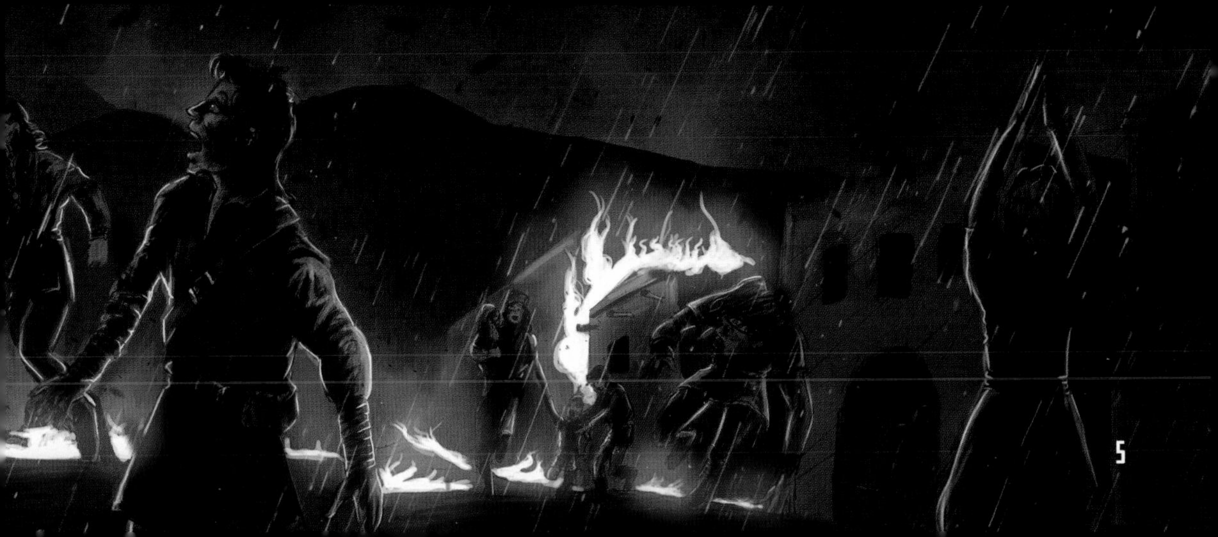

CHAPTER ONE

THE FOUR AGES OF MAN

A GREEK MYTH

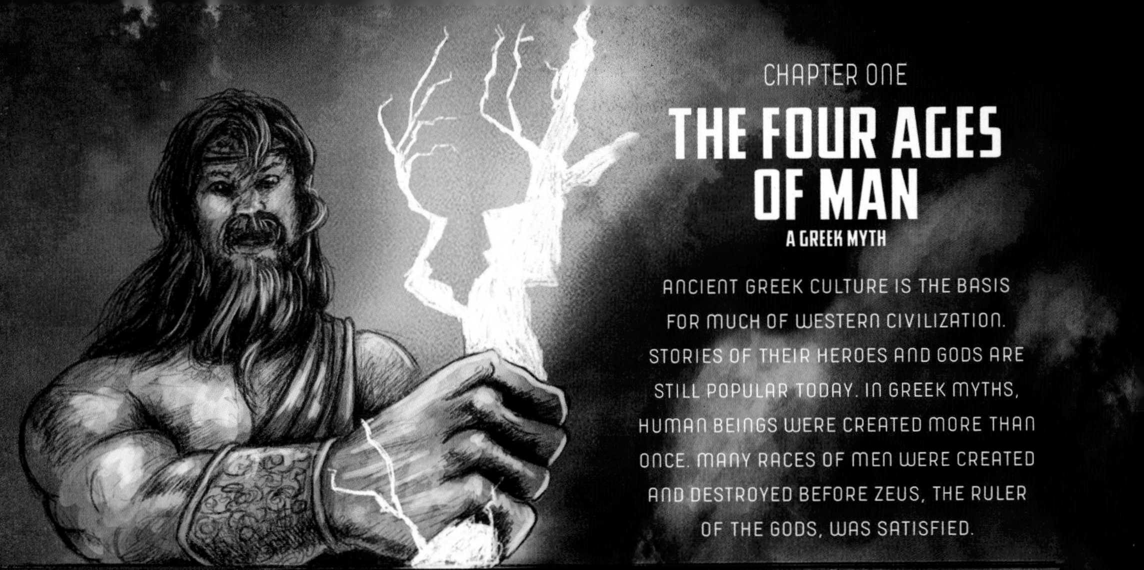

ANCIENT GREEK CULTURE IS THE BASIS FOR MUCH OF WESTERN CIVILIZATION. STORIES OF THEIR HEROES AND GODS ARE STILL POPULAR TODAY. IN GREEK MYTHS, HUMAN BEINGS WERE CREATED MORE THAN ONCE. MANY RACES OF MEN WERE CREATED AND DESTROYED BEFORE ZEUS, THE RULER OF THE GODS, WAS SATISFIED.

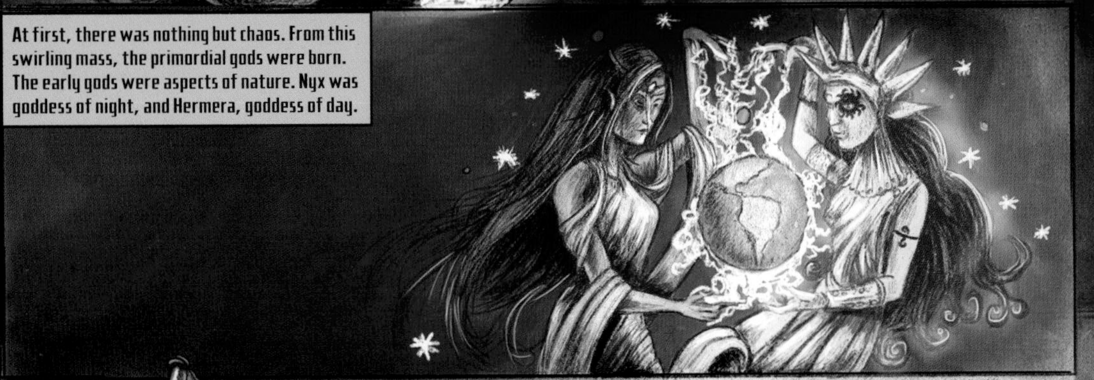
At first, there was nothing but chaos. From this swirling mass, the primordial gods were born. The early gods were aspects of nature. Nyx was goddess of night, and Hermera, goddess of day.

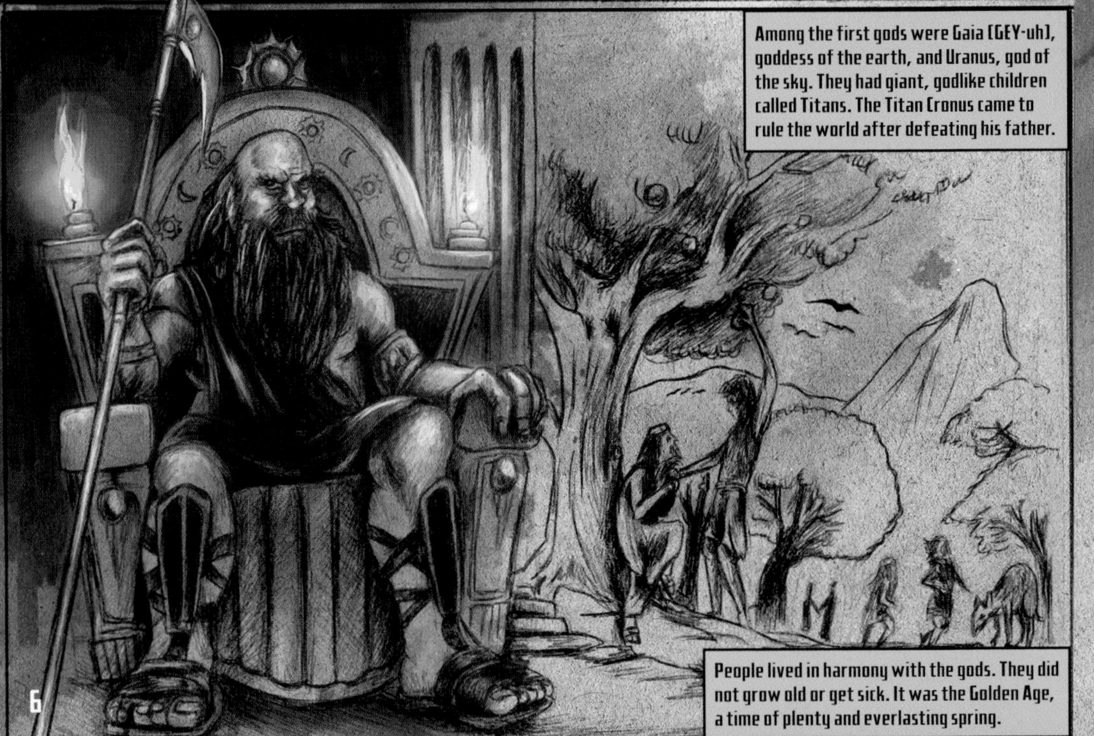
Among the first gods were Gaia [GEY-uh], goddess of the earth, and Uranus, god of the sky. They had giant, godlike children called Titans. The Titan Cronus came to rule the world after defeating his father.
People lived in harmony with the gods. They did not grow old or get sick. It was the Golden Age, a time of plenty and everlasting spring.

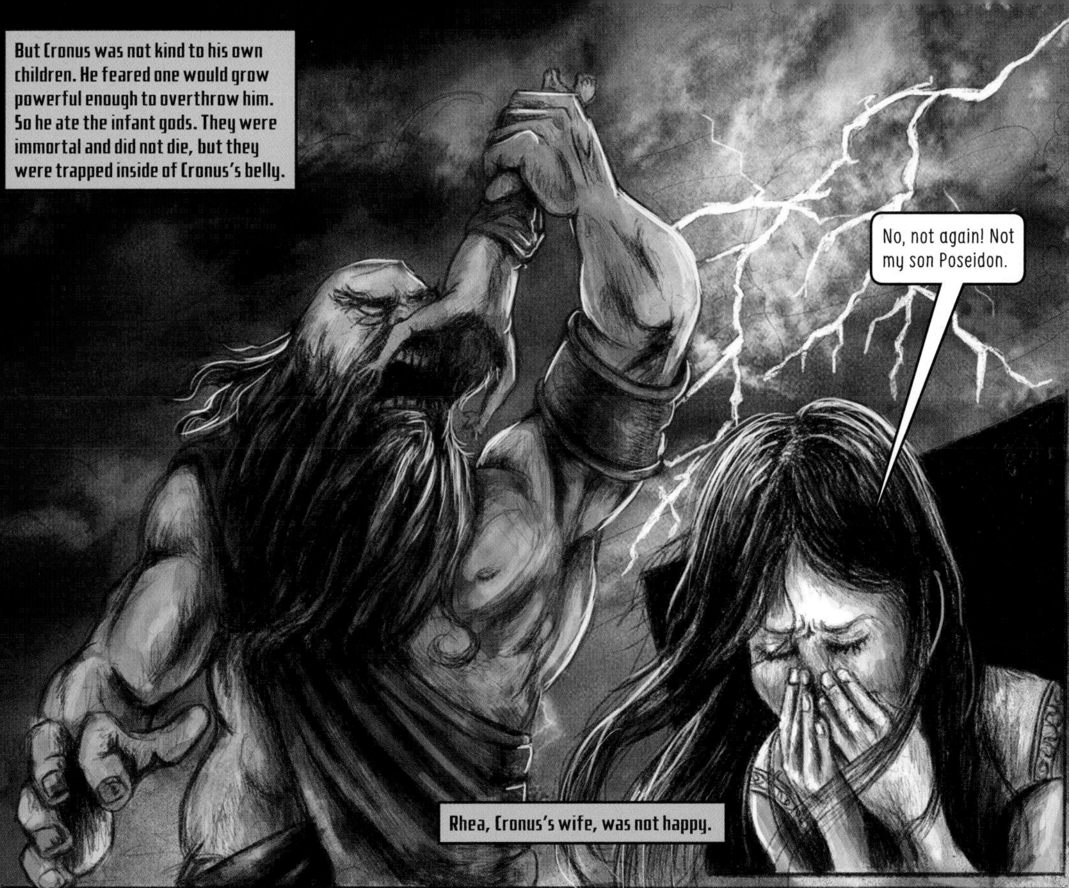
But Cronus was not kind to his own children. He feared one would grow powerful enough to overthrow him. So he ate the infant gods. They were immortal and did not die, but they were trapped inside of Cronus's belly.
No, not again! Not my son Poseidon.
Rhea, Cronus's wife, was not happy.

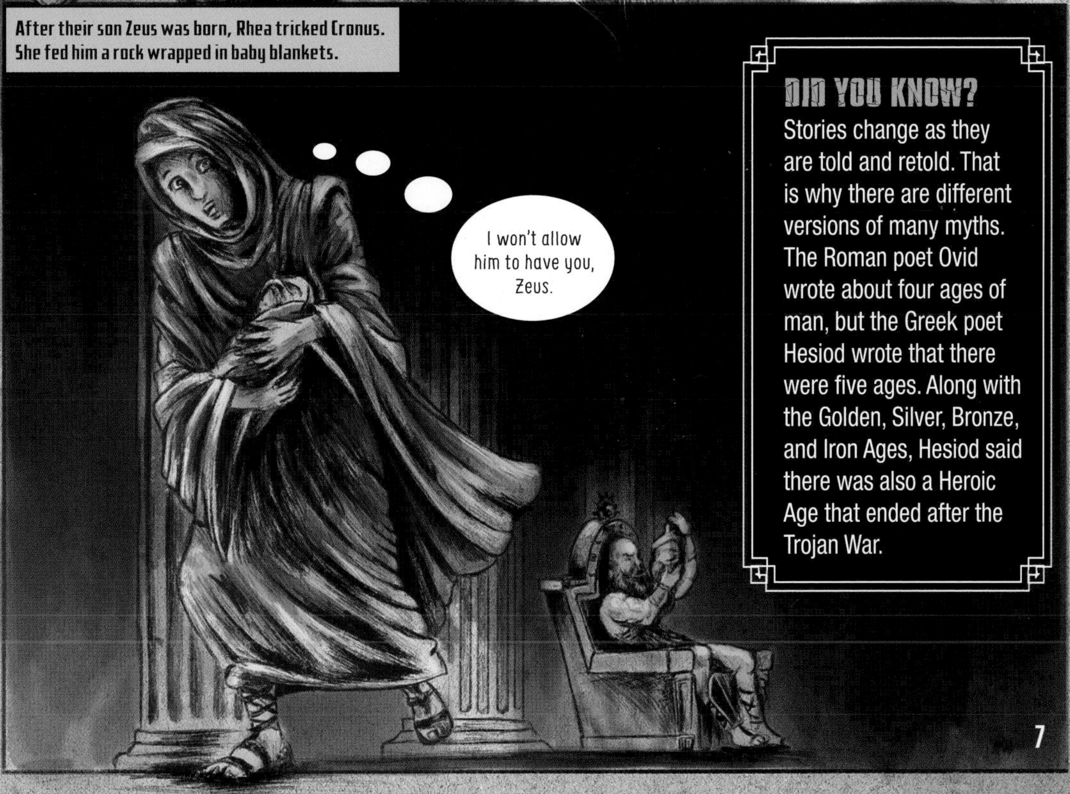
After their son Zeus was born, Rhea tricked Cronus. She fed him a rock wrapped in baby blankets.
I won't allow him to have you, Zeus.

DID YOU KNOW?

Stories change as they are told and retold. That is why there are different versions of many myths. The Roman poet Ovid wrote about four ages of man, but the Greek poet Hesiod wrote that there were five ages. Along with the Golden, Silver, Bronze, and Iron Ages, Hesiod said there was also a Heroic Age that ended after the Trojan War.

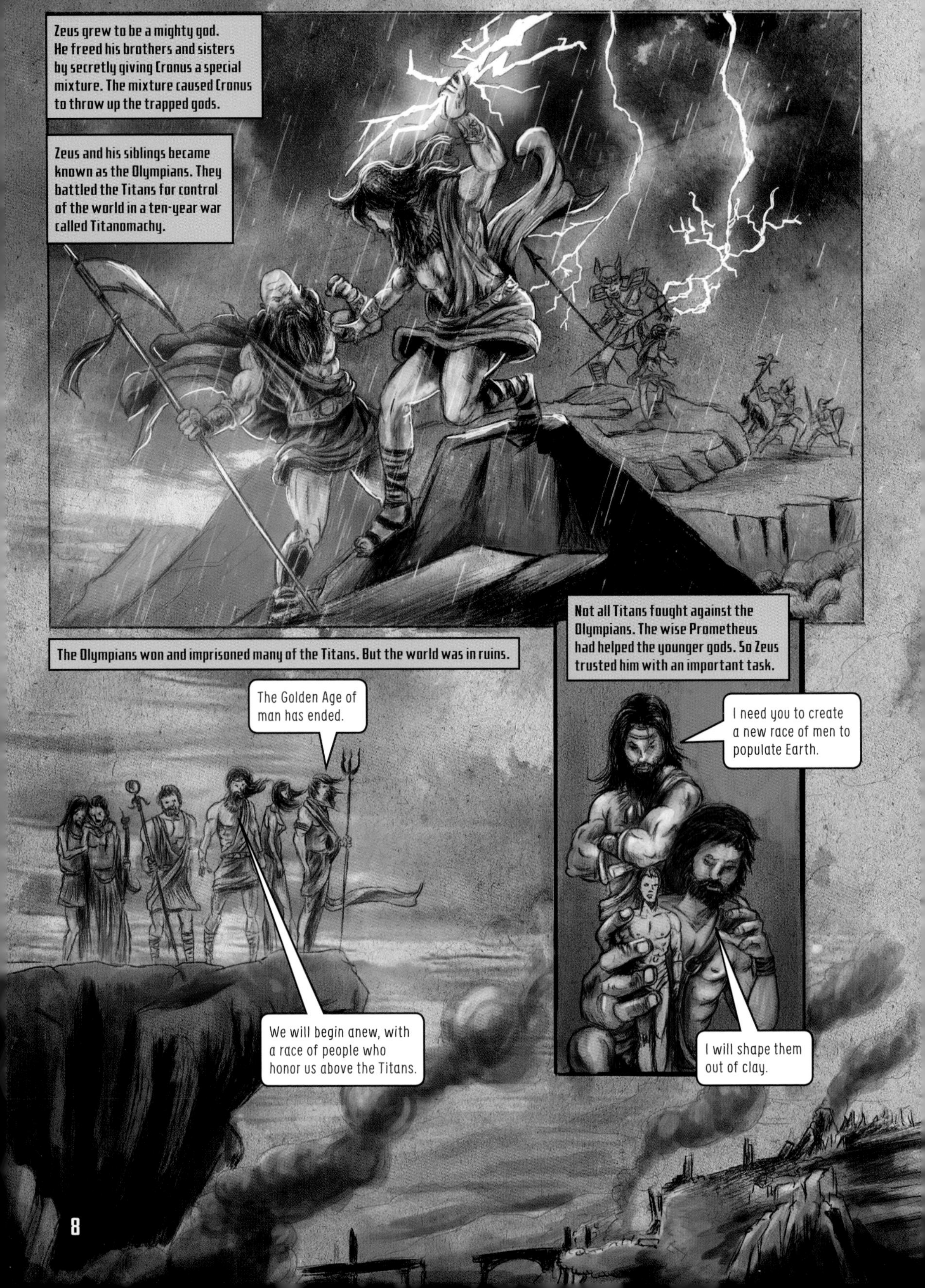
Zeus grew to be a mighty god. He freed his brothers and sisters by secretly giving Cronus a special mixture. The mixture caused Cronus to throw up the trapped gods.
Zeus and his siblings became known as the Olympians. They battled the Titans for control of the world in a ten-year war called Titanomachy.
The Olympians won and imprisoned many of the Titans. But the world was in ruins.
The Golden Age of man has ended.
We will begin anew, with a race of people who honor us above the Titans.
Not all Titans fought against the Olympians. The wise Prometheus had helped the younger gods. So Zeus trusted him with an important task.
I need you to create a new race of men to populate Earth.
I will shape them out of clay.

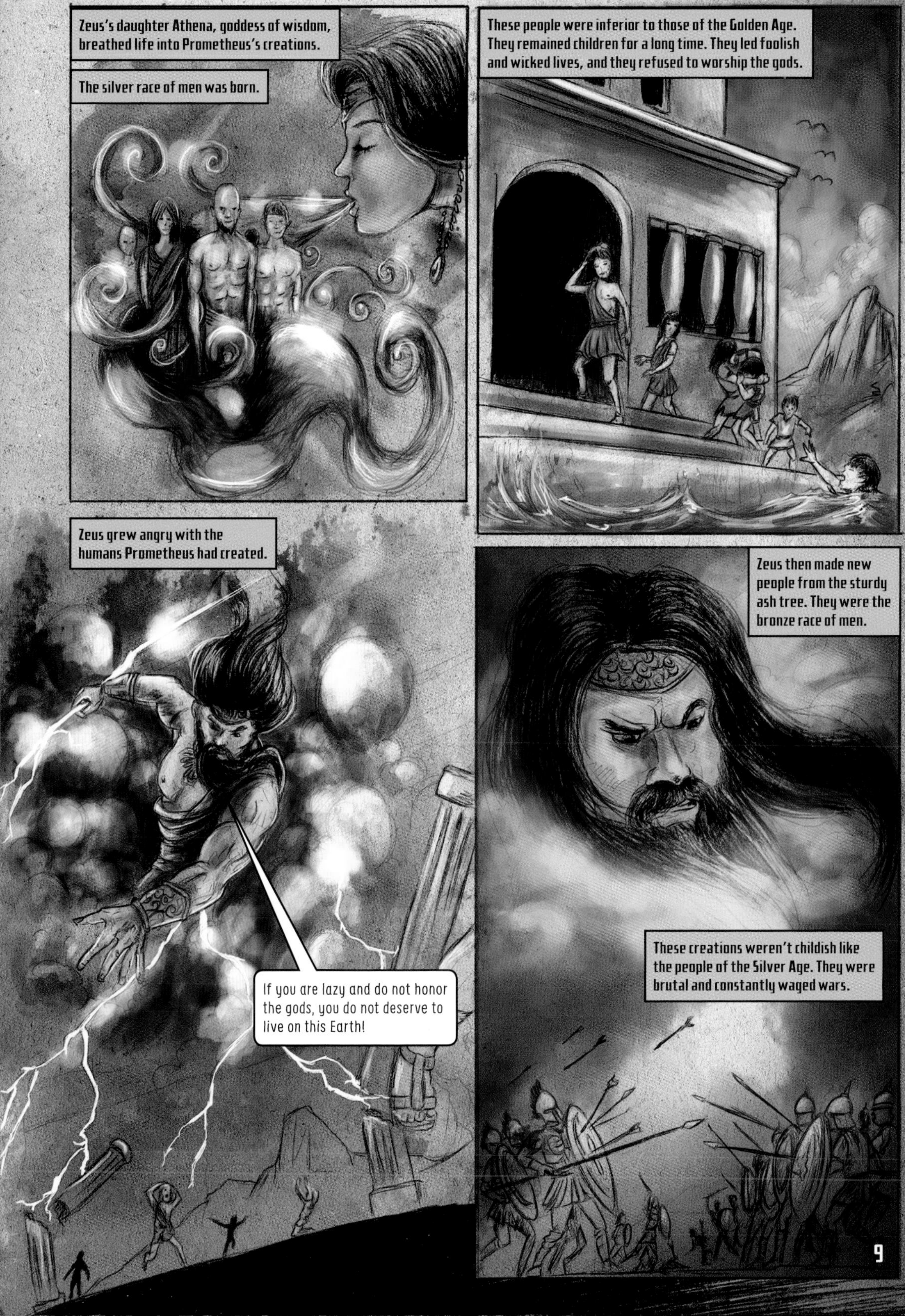

Zeus's daughter Athena, goddess of wisdom, breathed life into Prometheus's creations.
The silver race of men was born.
These people were inferior to those of the Golden Age. They remained children for a long time. They led foolish and wicked lives, and they refused to worship the gods.
Zeus grew angry with the humans Prometheus had created.
If you are lazy and do not honor the gods, you do not deserve to live on this Earth!
Zeus then made new people from the sturdy ash tree. They were the bronze race of men.
These creations weren't childish like the people of the Silver Age. They were brutal and constantly waged wars.

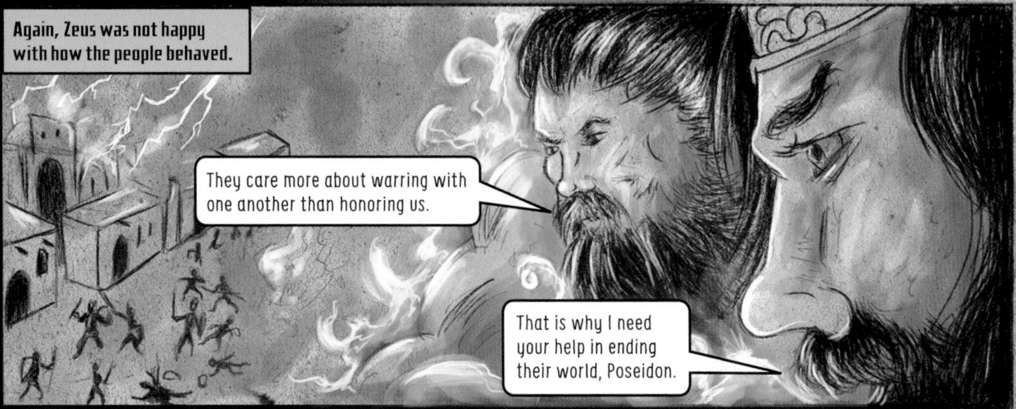
Again, Zeus was not happy with how the people behaved.
They care more about warring with one another than honoring us.
That is why I need your help in ending their world, Poseidon.

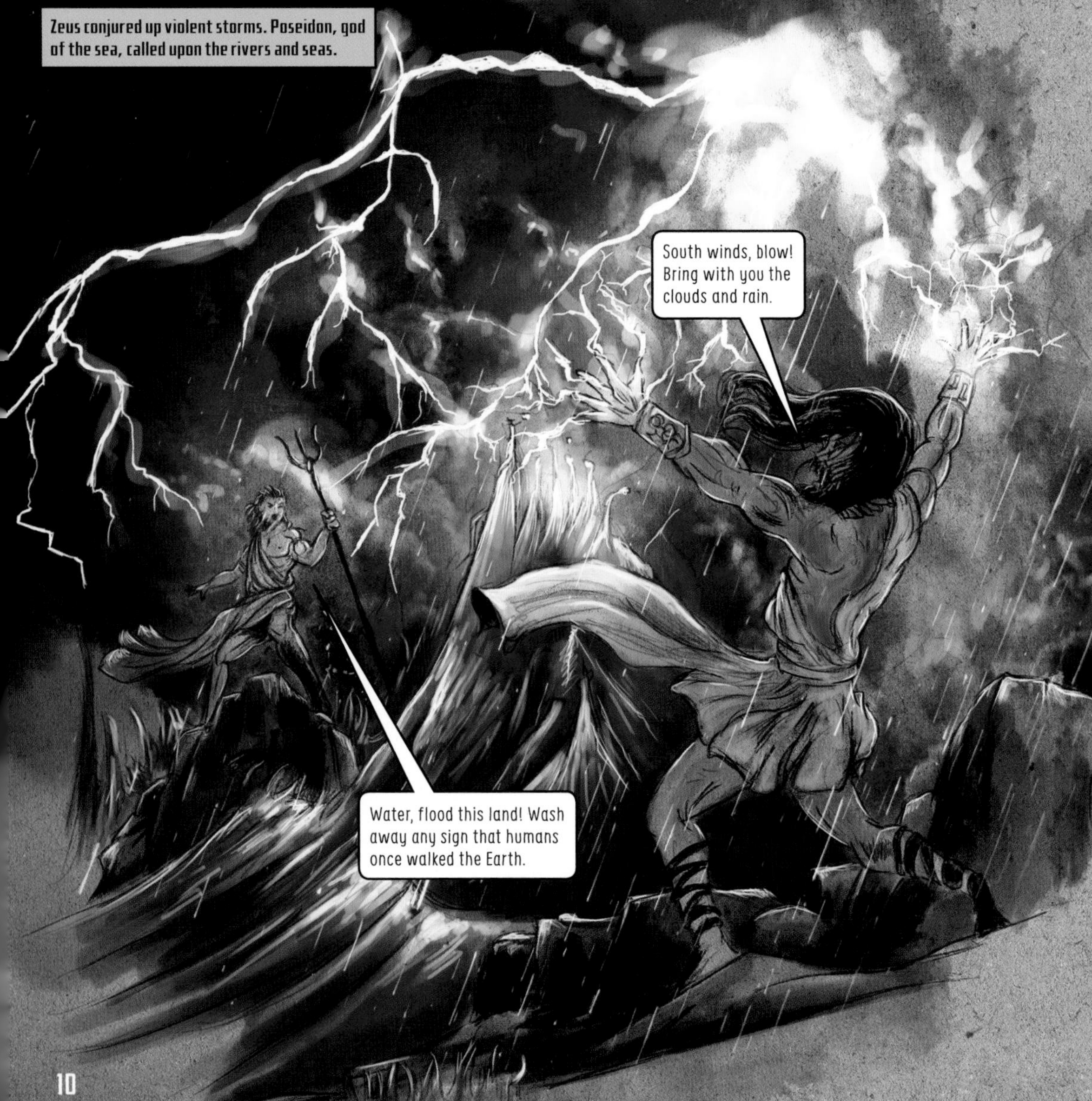
Zeus conjured up violent storms. Poseidon, god of the sea, called upon the rivers and seas.
South winds, blow! Bring with you the clouds and rain.
Water, flood this land! Wash away any sign that humans once walked the Earth.

The world was destroyed in the Great Deluge.

Yet two people named Deucalion and Pyrrha survived. Deucalion was the son of Prometheus. Before the flood, the Titan had warned his son and daughter-in-law of the coming danger. Prometheus had built a large wooden chest to keep the two safe.

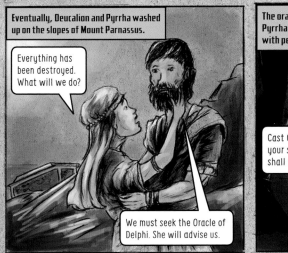

Eventually, Deucalion and Pyrrha washed up on the slopes of Mount Parnassus.

Everything has been destroyed. What will we do?

We must seek the Oracle of Delphi. She will advise us.

The oracle told Deucalion and Pyrrha how to fill the world with people again.

Cast Gaia's bones over your shoulders, and you shall repopulate the Earth.

Deucalion and Pyrrha guessed that the bones of Gaia, the goddess of earth, were rocks. Wherever Deucalion threw a stone, a man was born. Wherever Pyrrha threw one, a woman was born.

Thus the iron race of men came to be. According to the myths, it is the age we live in now.

But myths also warn that if the people of the Iron Age do not honor the gods, Zeus will return to wipe out all life once again.

CHAPTER TWO

ATUM THE GIANT SERPENT

AN EGYPTIAN MYTH

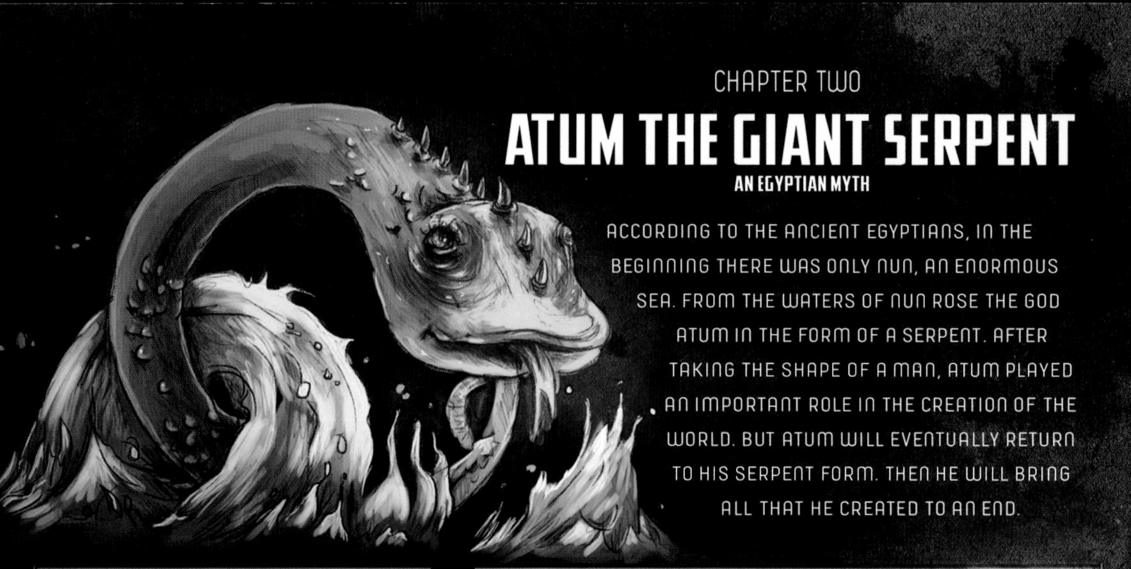

ACCORDING TO THE ANCIENT EGYPTIANS, IN THE BEGINNING THERE WAS ONLY NUN, AN ENORMOUS SEA. FROM THE WATERS OF NUN ROSE THE GOD ATUM IN THE FORM OF A SERPENT. AFTER TAKING THE SHAPE OF A MAN, ATUM PLAYED AN IMPORTANT ROLE IN THE CREATION OF THE WORLD. BUT ATUM WILL EVENTUALLY RETURN TO HIS SERPENT FORM. THEN HE WILL BRING ALL THAT HE CREATED TO AN END.

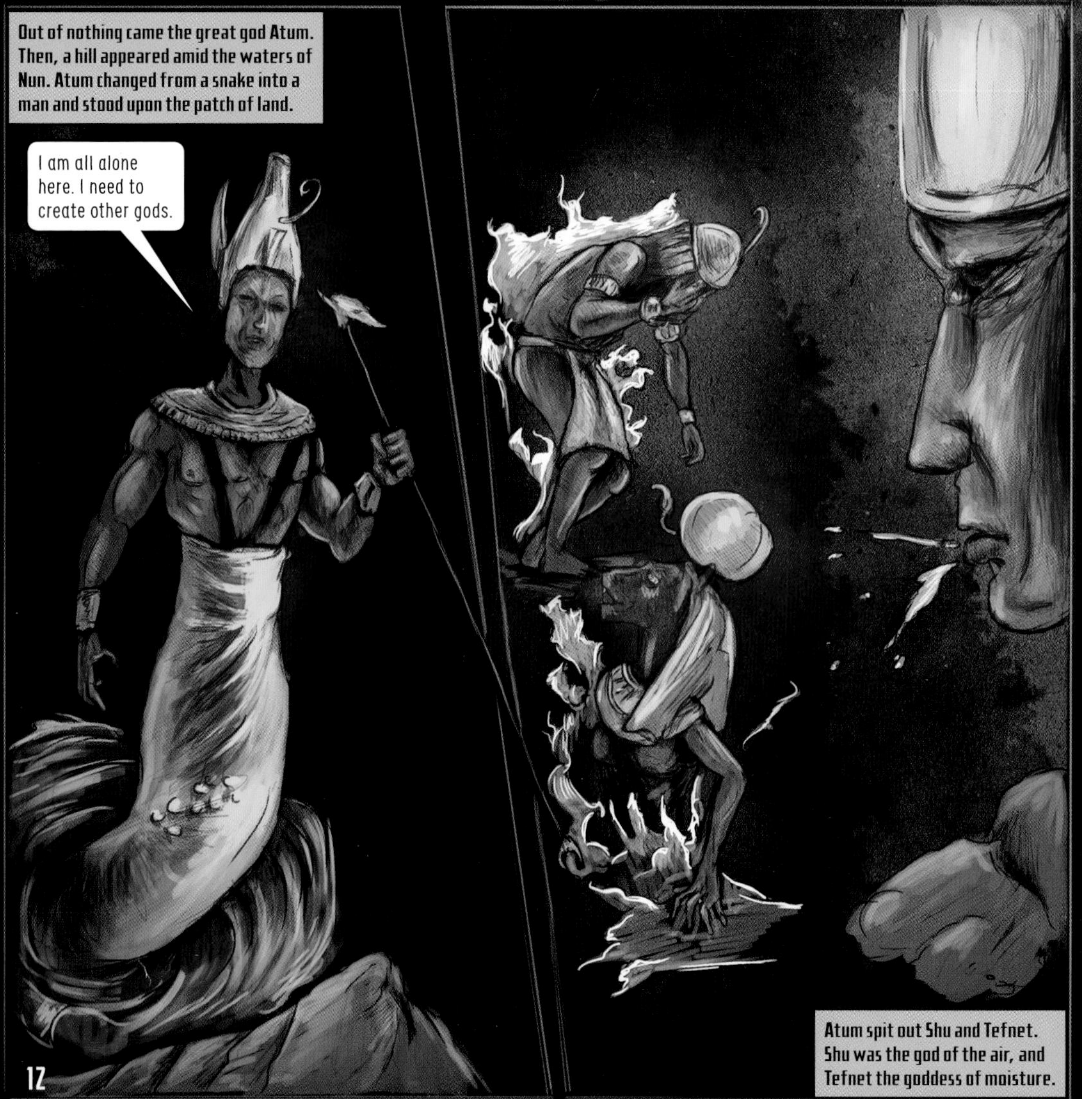
Out of nothing came the great god Atum. Then, a hill appeared amid the waters of Nun. Atum changed from a snake into a man and stood upon the patch of land.
I am all alone here. I need to create other gods.
Atum spit out Shu and Tefnet. Shu was the god of the air, and Tefnet the goddess of moisture.

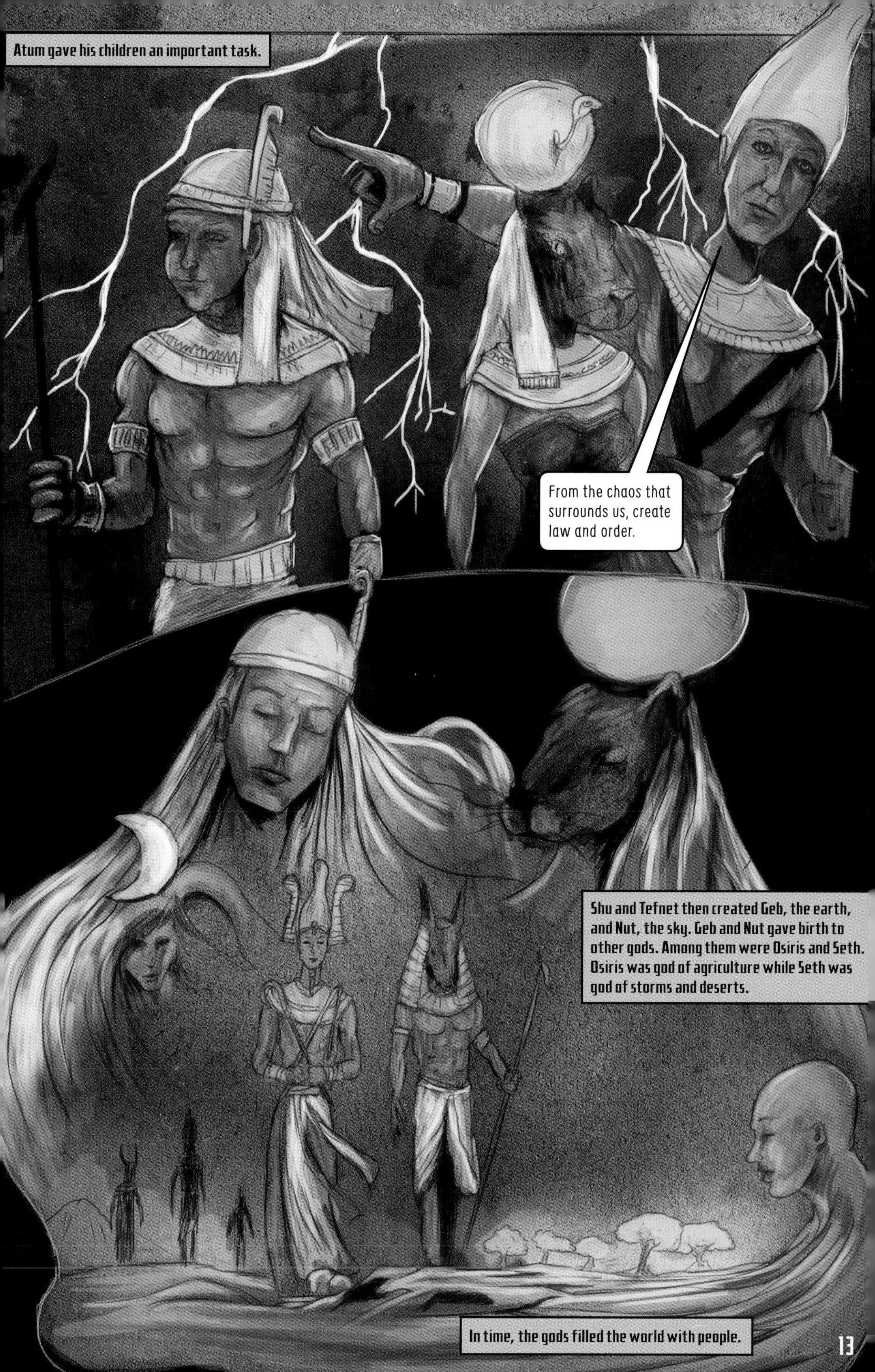
Atum gave his children an important task.
From the chaos that surrounds us, create law and order.
Shu and Tefnet then created Geb, the earth, and Nut, the sky. Geb and Nut gave birth to other gods. Among them were Osiris and Seth. Osiris was god of agriculture while Seth was god of storms and deserts.
In time, the gods filled the world with people.

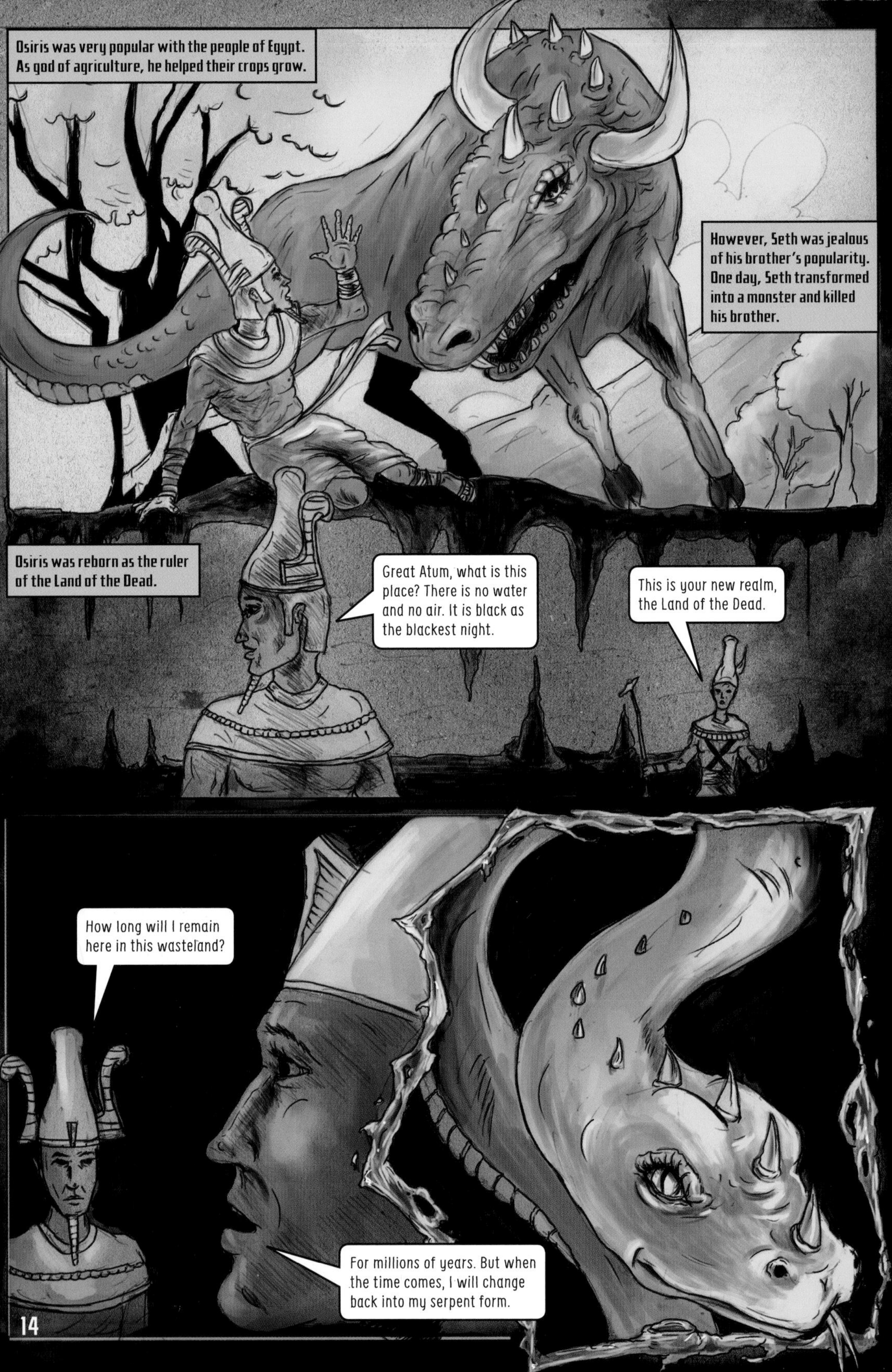

Osiris was very popular with the people of Egypt. As god of agriculture, he helped their crops grow.
However, Seth was jealous of his brother's popularity. One day, Seth transformed into a monster and killed his brother.
Osiris was reborn as the ruler of the Land of the Dead.
Great Atum, what is this place? There is no water and no air. It is black as the blackest night.
This is your new realm, the Land of the Dead.
How long will I remain here in this wasteland?
For millions of years. But when the time comes, I will change back into my serpent form.

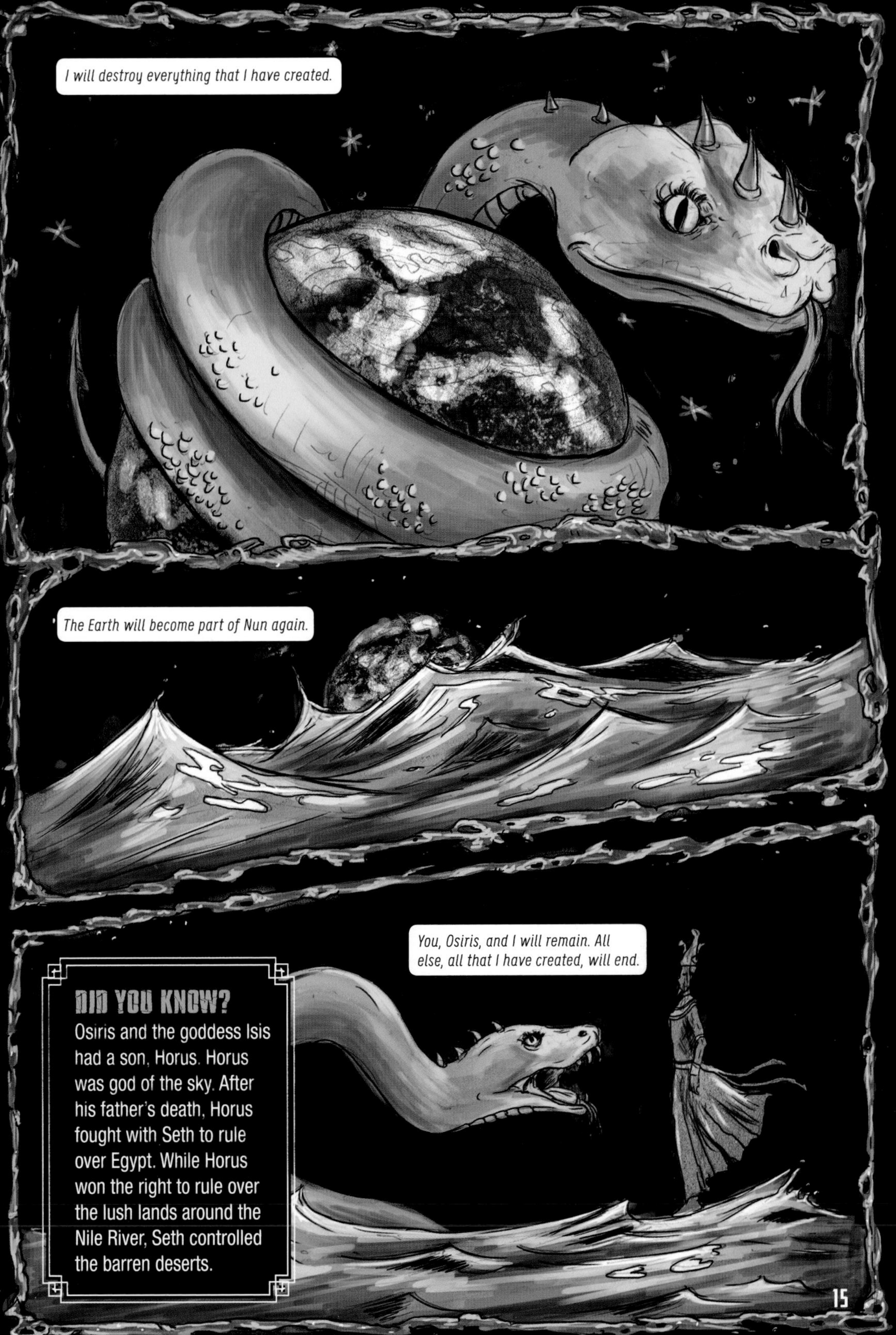
I will destroy everything that I have created.
The Earth will become part of Nun again.
You, Osiris, and I will remain. All else, all that I have created, will end.

DID YOU KNOW?

Osiris and the goddess Isis had a son, Horus. Horus was god of the sky. After his father's death, Horus fought with Seth to rule over Egypt. While Horus won the right to rule over the lush lands around the Nile River, Seth controlled the barren deserts.

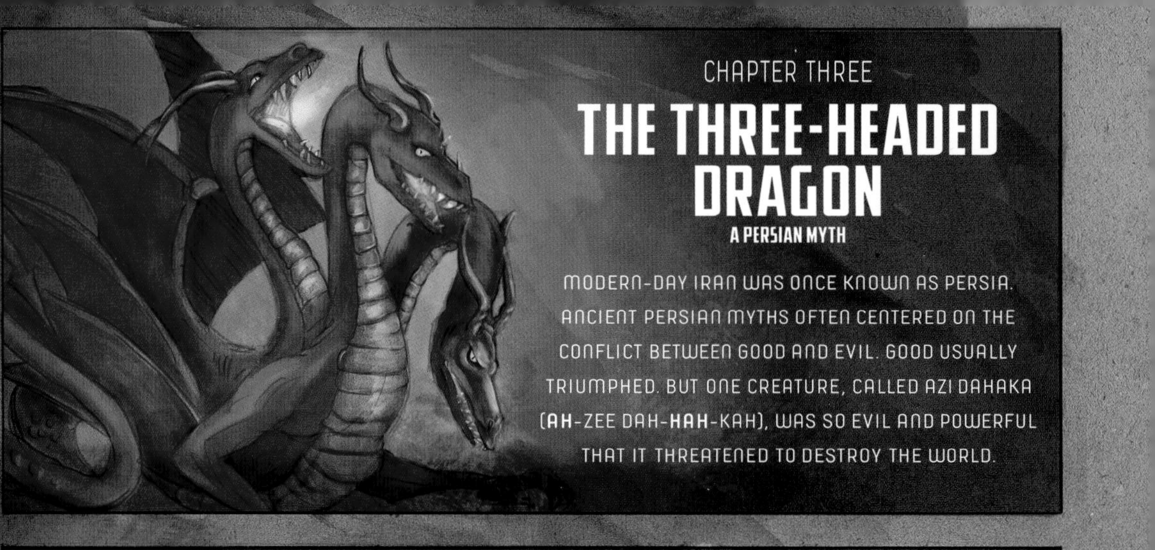

CHAPTER THREE

THE THREE-HEADED DRAGON

A PERSIAN MYTH

MODERN-DAY IRAN WAS ONCE KNOWN AS PERSIA. ANCIENT PERSIAN MYTHS OFTEN CENTERED ON THE CONFLICT BETWEEN GOOD AND EVIL. GOOD USUALLY TRIUMPHED. BUT ONE CREATURE, CALLED AZI DAHAKA (**AH**-ZEE DAH-**HAH**-KAH), WAS SO EVIL AND POWERFUL THAT IT THREATENED TO DESTROY THE WORLD.

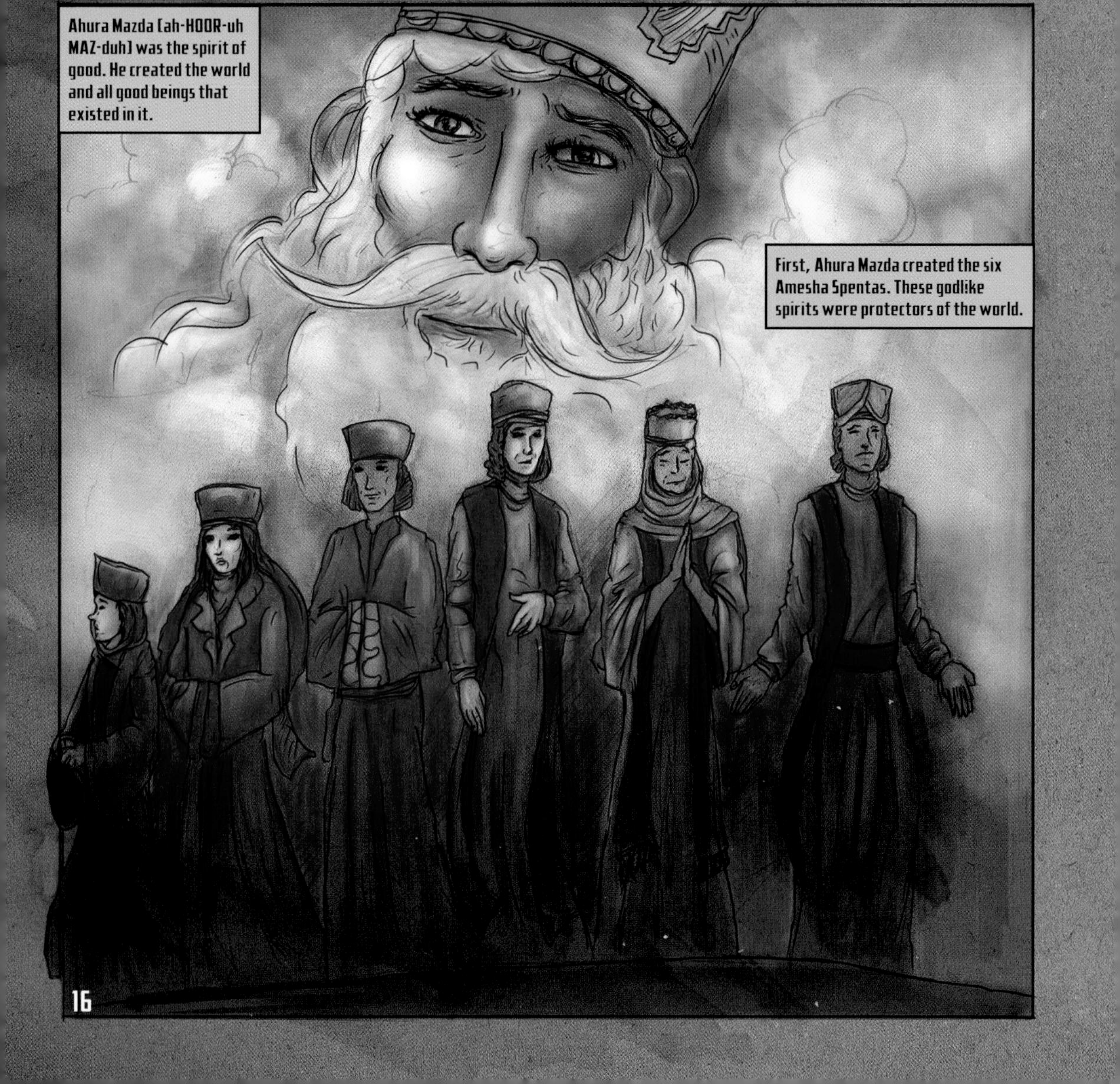
Ahura Mazda (ah-HOOR-uh MAZ-duh) was the spirit of good. He created the world and all good beings that existed in it.
First, Ahura Mazda created the six Amesha Spentas. These godlike spirits were protectors of the world.

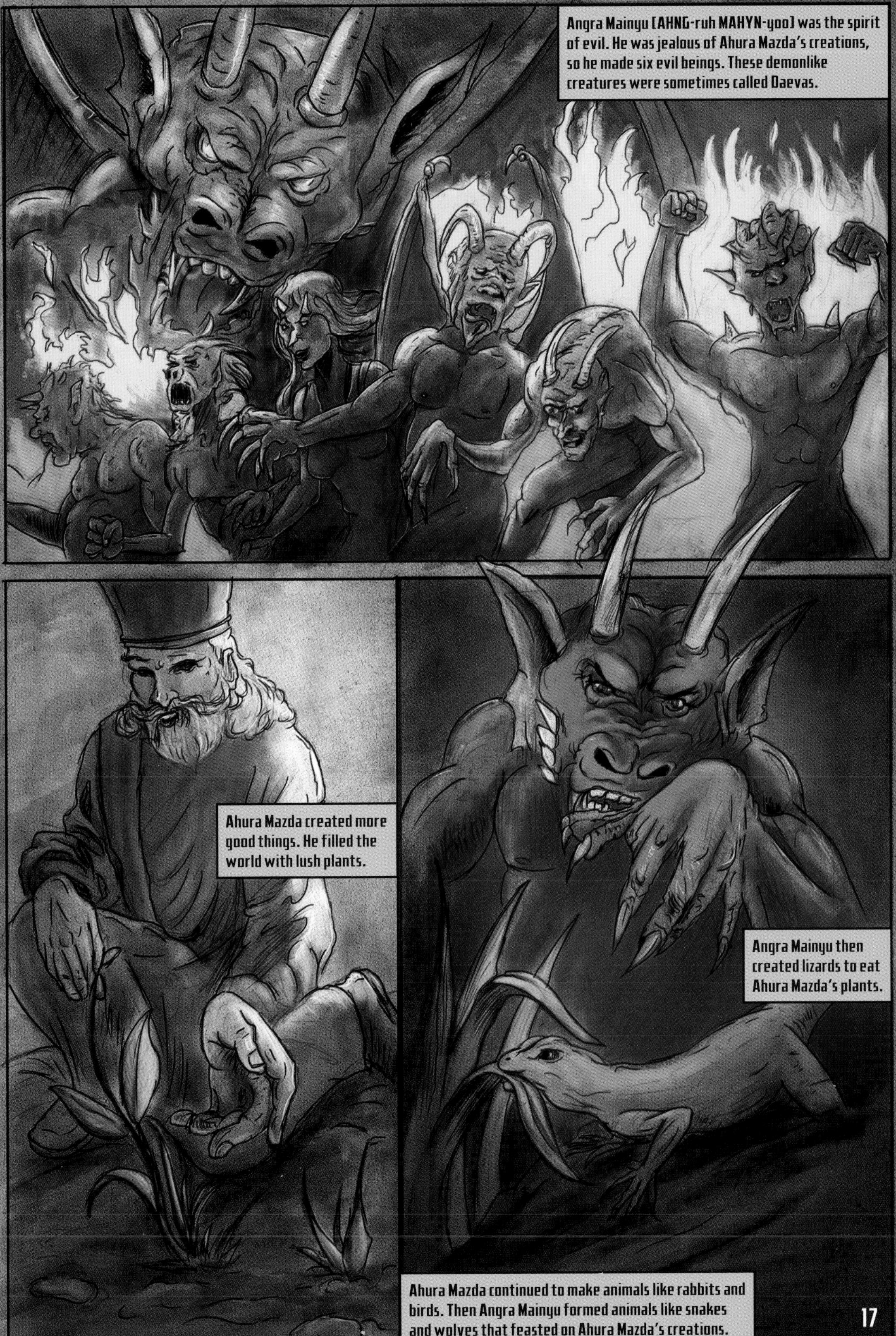
Angra Mainyu [AHNG-ruh MAHYN-yoo] was the spirit of evil. He was jealous of Ahura Mazda's creations, so he made six evil beings. These demonlike creatures were sometimes called Daevas.
Ahura Mazda created more good things. He filled the world with lush plants.
Angra Mainyu then created lizards to eat Ahura Mazda's plants.
Ahura Mazda continued to make animals like rabbits and birds. Then Angra Mainyu formed animals like snakes and wolves that feasted on Ahura Mazda's creations.

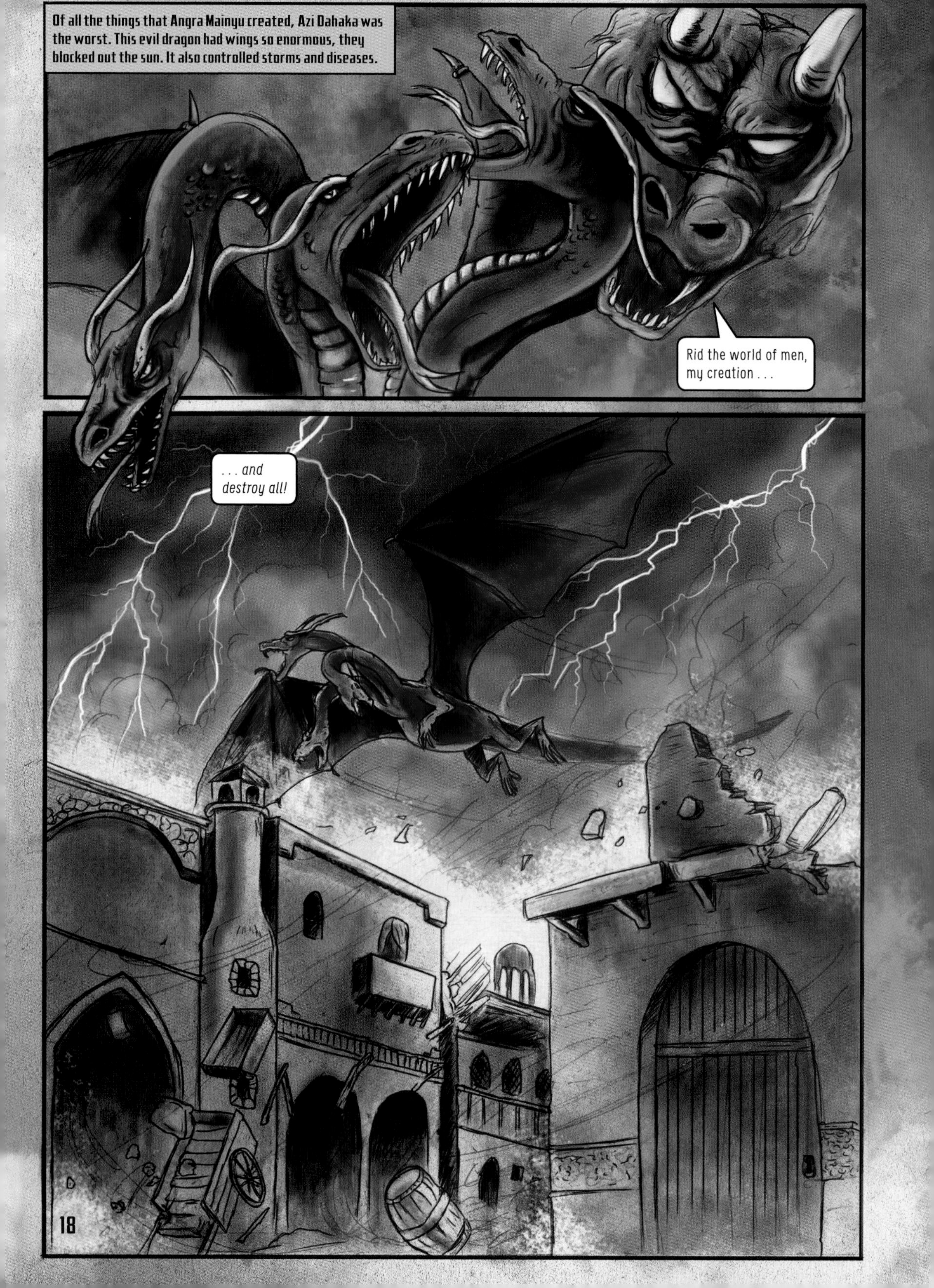
Of all the things that Angra Mainyu created, Azi Dahaka was the worst. This evil dragon had wings so enormous, they blocked out the sun. It also controlled storms and diseases.
Rid the world of men, my creation . . .
. . . and destroy all!

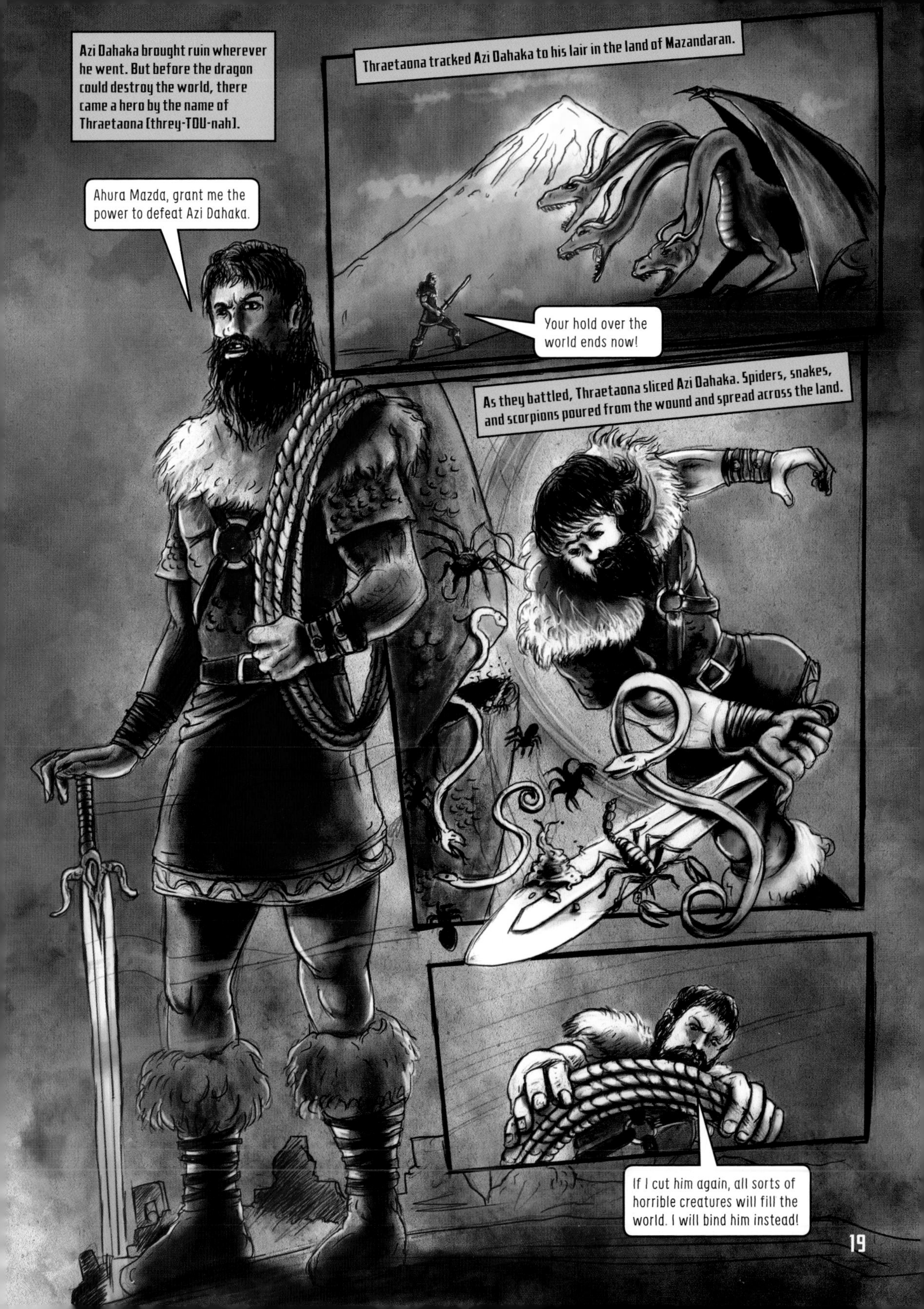

Azi Dahaka brought ruin wherever he went. But before the dragon could destroy the world, there came a hero by the name of Thraetaona [threy-TOU-nah].
Ahura Mazda, grant me the power to defeat Azi Dahaka.
Thraetaona tracked Azi Dahaka to his lair in the land of Mazandaran.
Your hold over the world ends now!
As they battled, Thraetaona sliced Azi Dahaka. Spiders, snakes, and scorpions poured from the wound and spread across the land.
If I cut him again, all sorts of horrible creatures will fill the world. I will bind him instead!

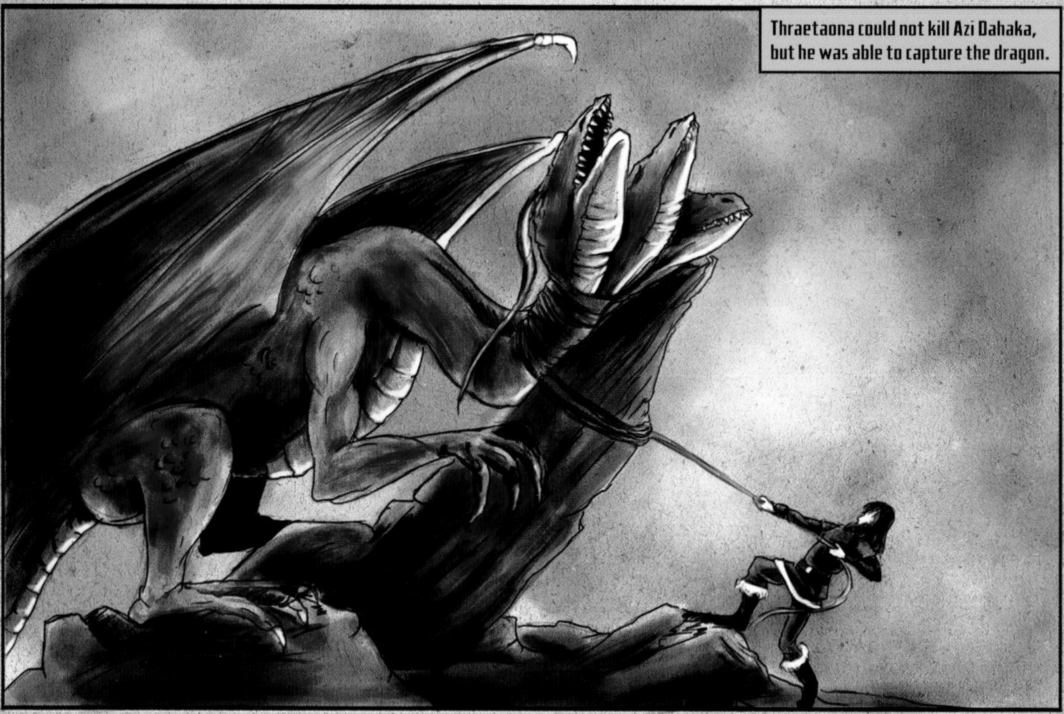
Thraetaona could not kill Azi Dahaka, but he was able to capture the dragon.

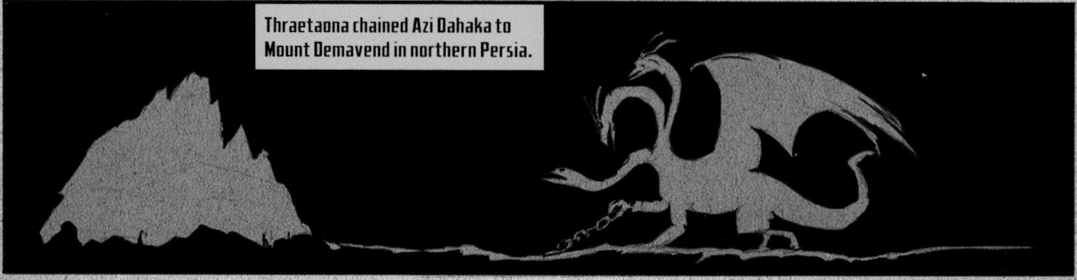
Thraetaona chained Azi Dahaka to Mount Demavend in northern Persia.

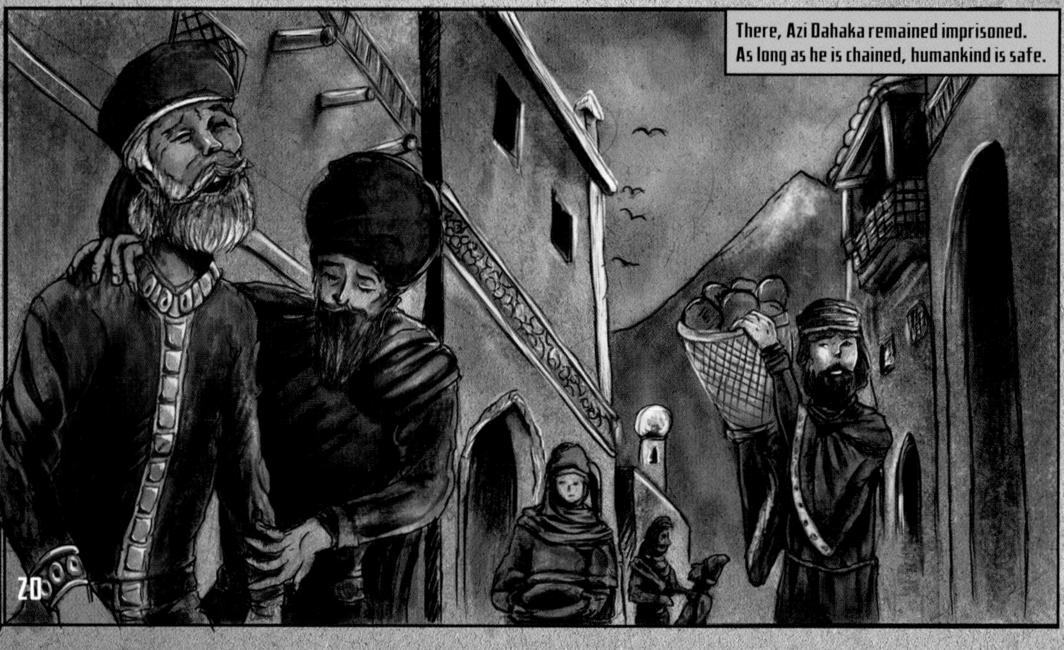
There, Azi Dahaka remained imprisoned. As long as he is chained, humankind is safe.

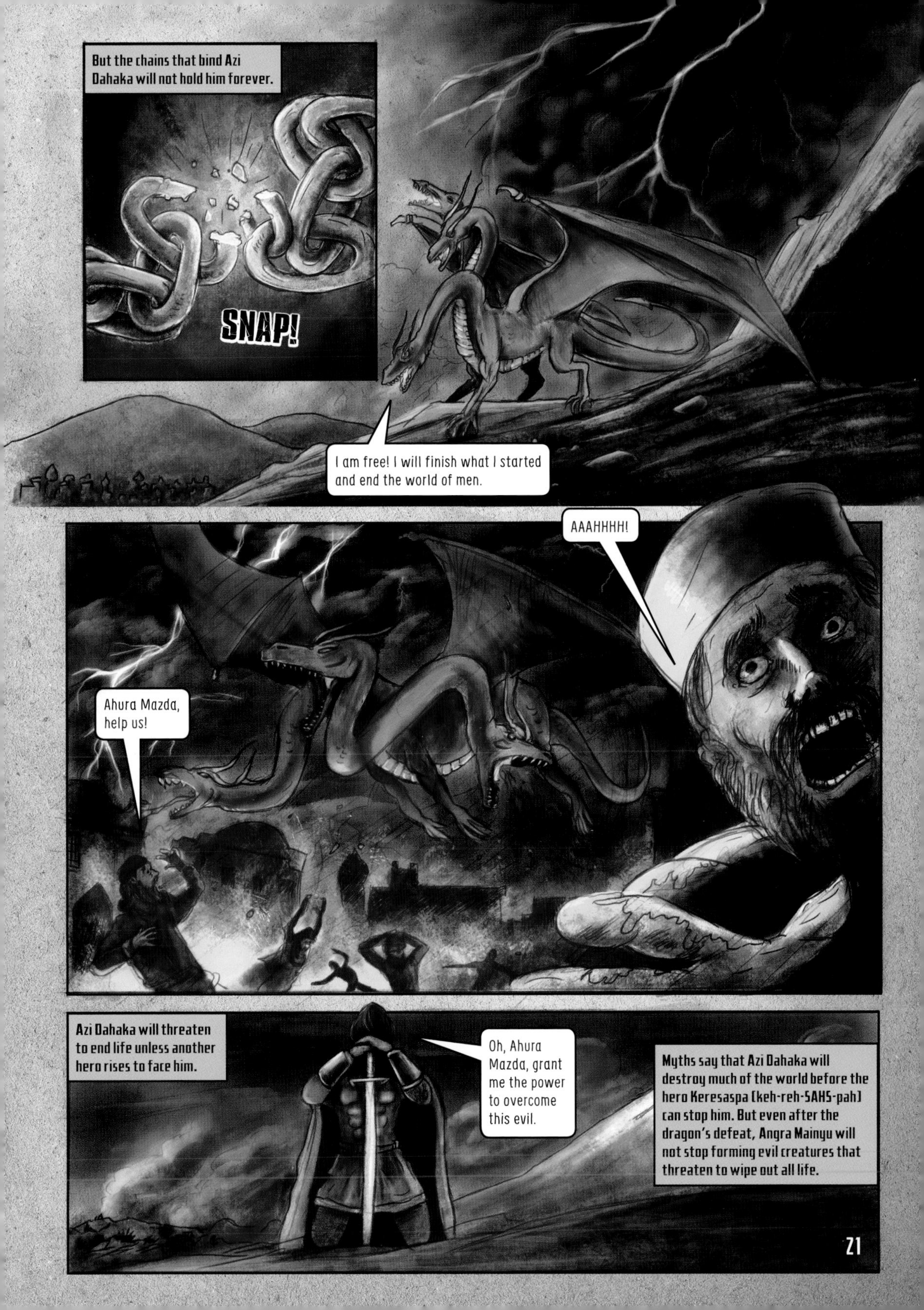
But the chains that bind Azi Dahaka will not hold him forever.
SNAP!
I am free! I will finish what I started and end the world of men.
AAAHHHH!
Ahura Mazda, help us!
Azi Dahaka will threaten to end life unless another hero rises to face him.
Oh, Ahura Mazda, grant me the power to overcome this evil.
Myths say that Azi Dahaka will destroy much of the world before the hero Keresaspa (keh-reh-SAHS-pah) can stop him. But even after the dragon's defeat, Angra Mainyu will not stop forming evil creatures that threaten to wipe out all life.

CHAPTER FOUR

RAGNAROK

A NORSE MYTH

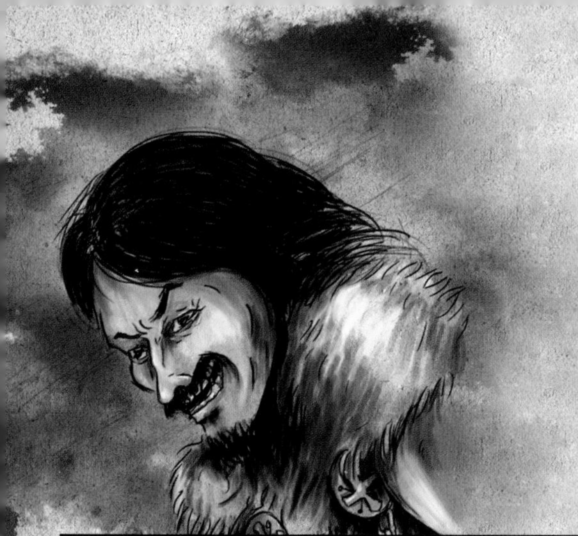

NORSE MYTHS OFTEN FOCUS ON BATTLES BETWEEN TWO RIVAL GROUPS — THE GIANTS AND THE AESIR (**EY**-SIR) GODS. AFTER ONE DEADLY FIGHT, ODIN, THE LEADER OF THE AESIR, TOOK A GIANT'S SON AND RAISED HIM AMONG THE GODS. THE BOY'S NAME WAS LOKI. BUT LOKI, THE GOD OF MISCHIEF, DID NOT ALWAYS GET ALONG WITH THE AESIR. ONE DAY, LOKI WILL HELP BRING ABOUT RAGNAROK, THE DESTRUCTION OF THE WORLD.

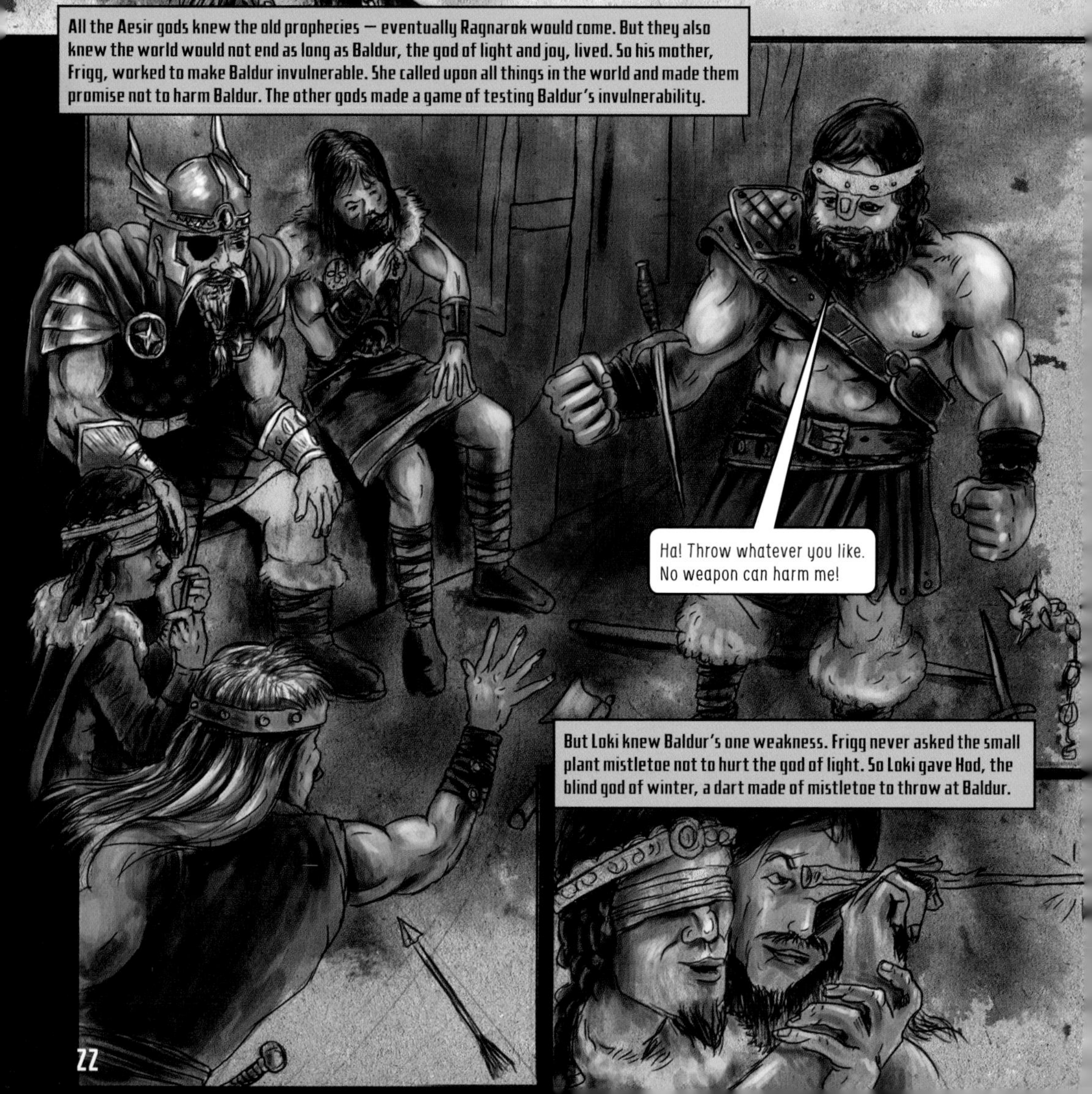
All the Aesir gods knew the old prophecies — eventually Ragnarok would come. But they also knew the world would not end as long as Baldur, the god of light and joy, lived. So his mother, Frigg, worked to make Baldur invulnerable. She called upon all things in the world and made them promise not to harm Baldur. The other gods made a game of testing Baldur's invulnerability.
Ha! Throw whatever you like. No weapon can harm me!
But Loki knew Baldur's one weakness. Frigg never asked the small plant mistletoe not to hurt the god of light. So Loki gave Hod, the blind god of winter, a dart made of mistletoe to throw at Baldur.

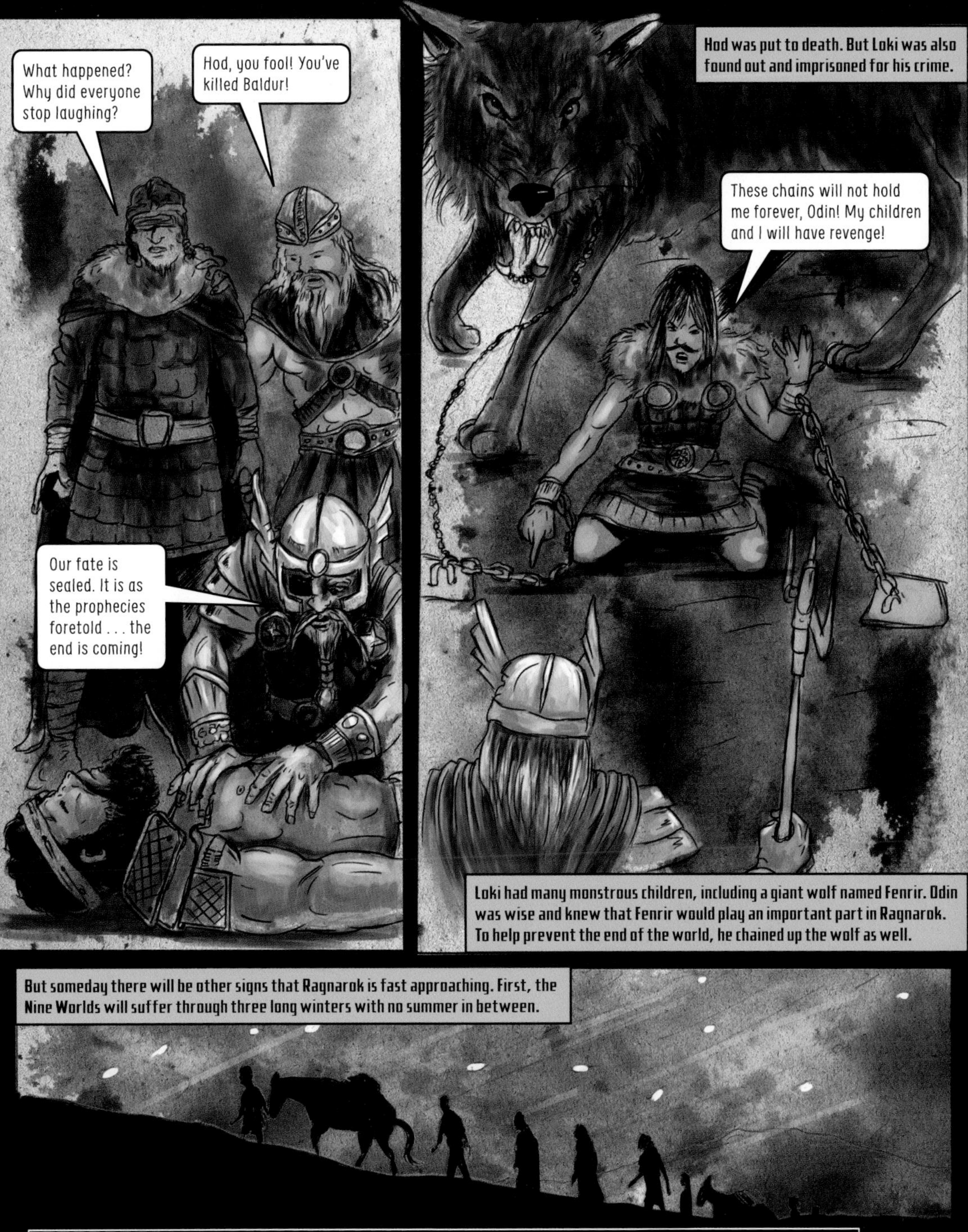
What happened? Why did everyone stop laughing?
Hod, you fool! You've killed Baldur!
Our fate is sealed. It is as the prophecies foretold . . . the end is coming!
Hod was put to death. But Loki was also found out and imprisoned for his crime.
These chains will not hold me forever, Odin! My children and I will have revenge!
Loki had many monstrous children, including a giant wolf named Fenrir. Odin was wise and knew that Fenrir would play an important part in Ragnarok. To help prevent the end of the world, he chained up the wolf as well.
But someday there will be other signs that Ragnarok is fast approaching. First, the Nine Worlds will suffer through three long winters with no summer in between.

DID YOU KNOW?

There are nine worlds in Norse mythology. Asgard is home to the Aesir gods, and Vanaheim is home to the Vanir gods. Jotunheim is the world of giants. Midgard is where humans dwell. Elves live on Alfheim, and dwarves on Svartalfheim. Niflheim is a world of ice while Muspelheim is a world of fire. Hel is the underworld. The Nine Worlds are connected by the tree of life, called Yggdrasil.

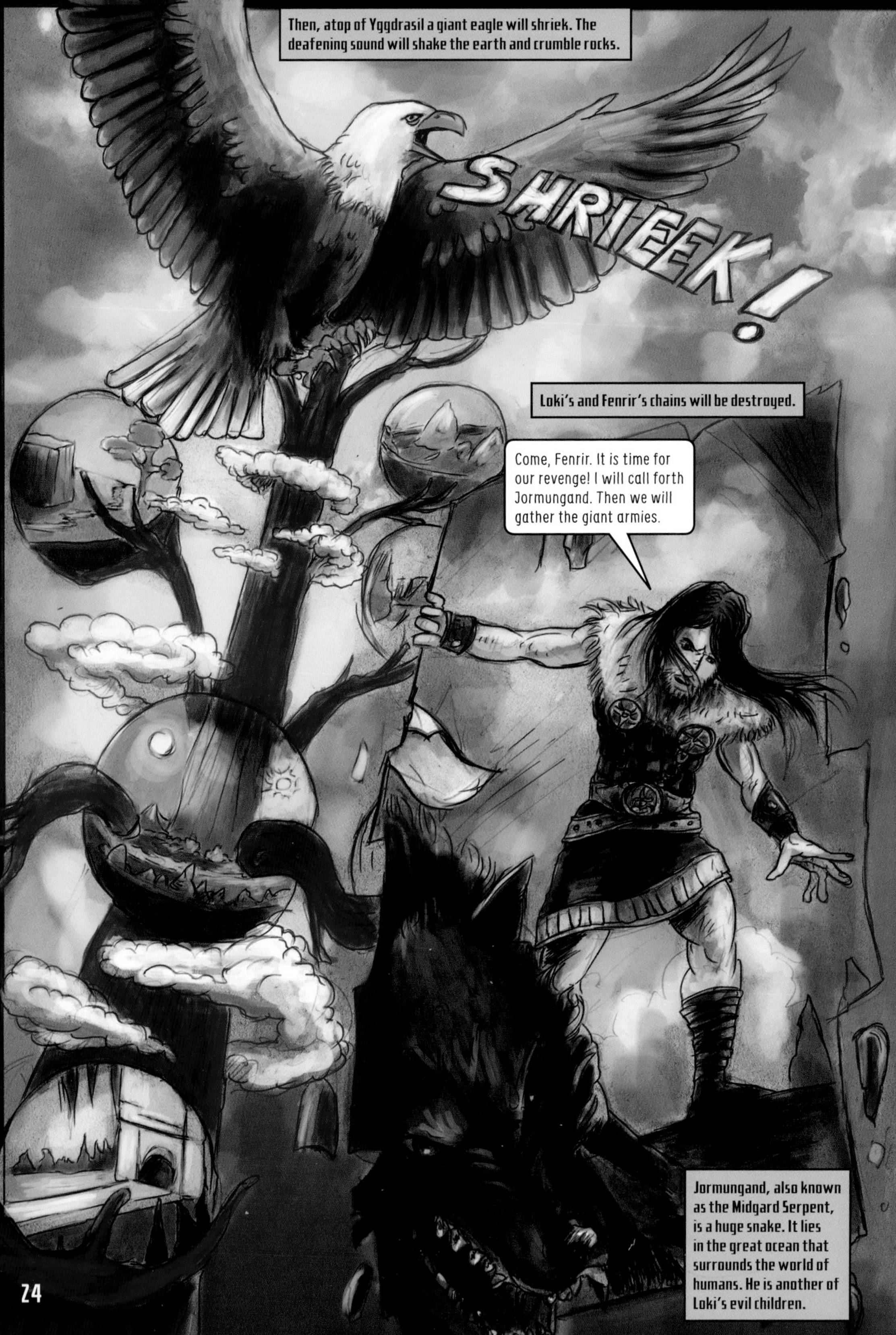
Then, atop of Yggdrasil a giant eagle will shriek. The deafening sound will shake the earth and crumble rocks.
SHRIEEK!
Loki's and Fenrir's chains will be destroyed.
Come, Fenrir. It is time for our revenge! I will call forth Jormungand. Then we will gather the giant armies.
Jormungand, also known as the Midgard Serpent, is a huge snake. It lies in the great ocean that surrounds the world of humans. He is another of Loki's evil children.

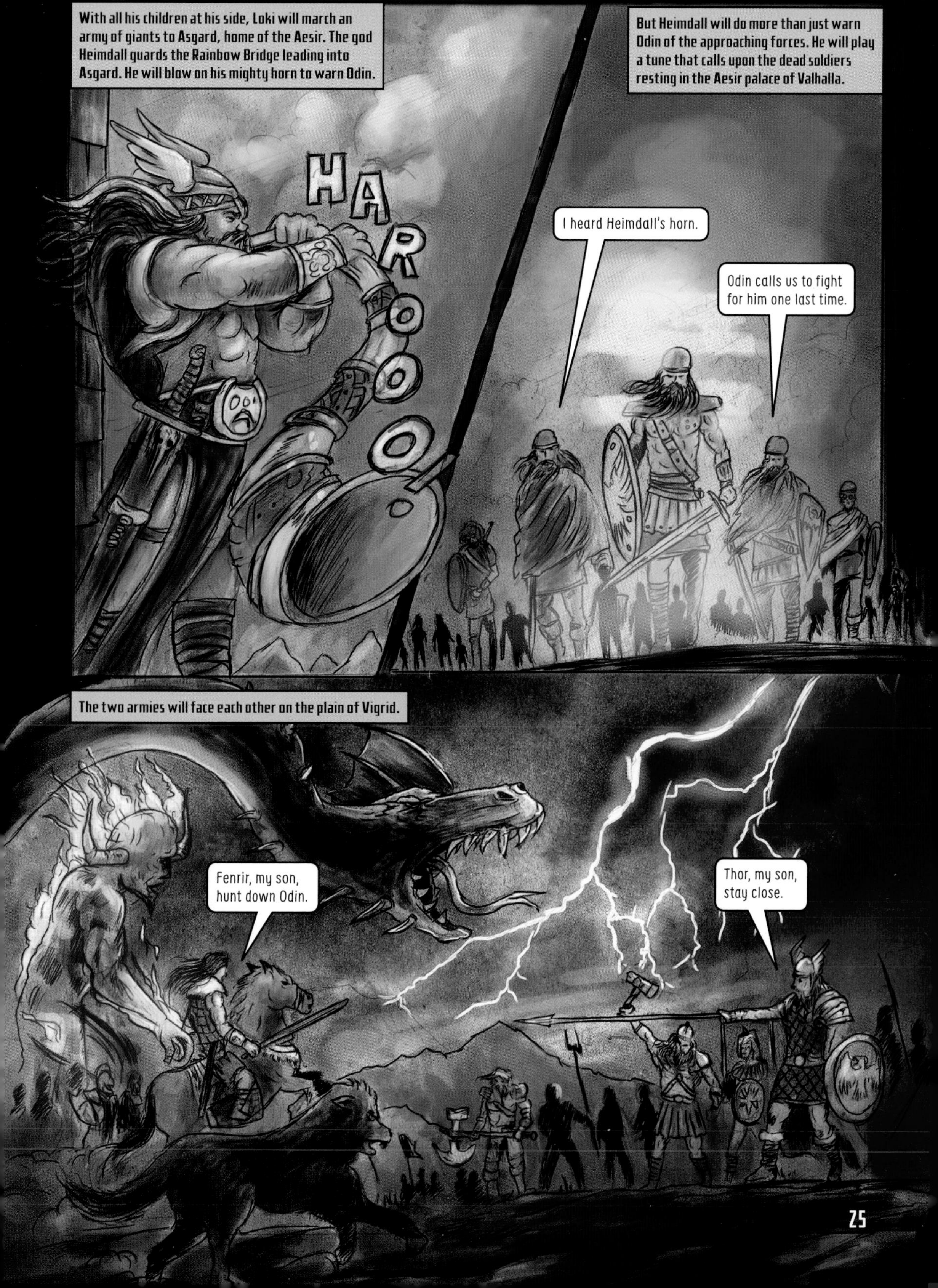
With all his children at his side, Loki will march an army of giants to Asgard, home of the Aesir. The god Heimdall guards the Rainbow Bridge leading into Asgard. He will blow on his mighty horn to warn Odin.
HAROOOO
But Heimdall will do more than just warn Odin of the approaching forces. He will play a tune that calls upon the dead soldiers resting in the Aesir palace of Valhalla.
I heard Heimdall's horn.
Odin calls us to fight for him one last time.
The two armies will face each other on the plain of Vigrid.
Fenrir, my son, hunt down Odin.
Thor, my son, stay close.

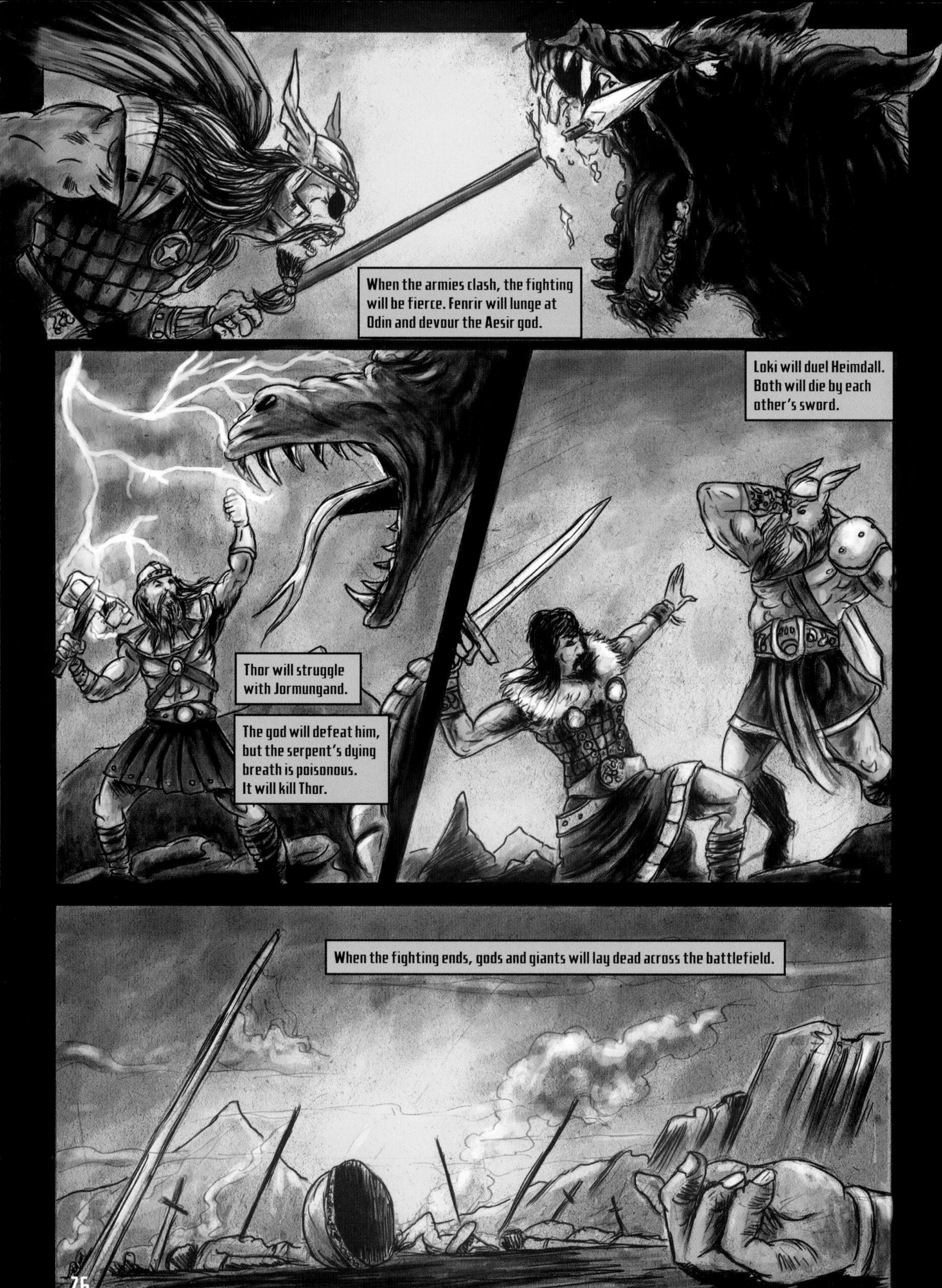

When the armies clash, the fighting will be fierce. Fenrir will lunge at Odin and devour the Aesir god.
Thor will struggle with Jormungand.
The god will defeat him, but the serpent's dying breath is poisonous. It will kill Thor.
Loki will duel Heimdall. Both will die by each other's sword.
When the fighting ends, gods and giants will lay dead across the battlefield.

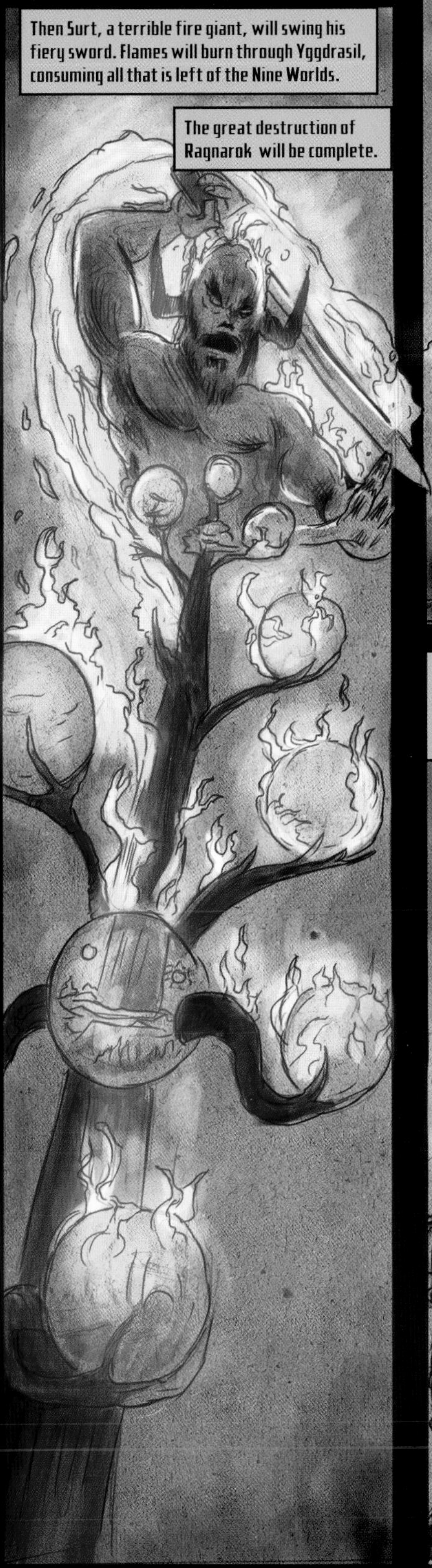
Then Surt, a terrible fire giant, will swing his fiery sword. Flames will burn through Yggdrasil, consuming all that is left of the Nine Worlds.
The great destruction of Ragnarok will be complete.

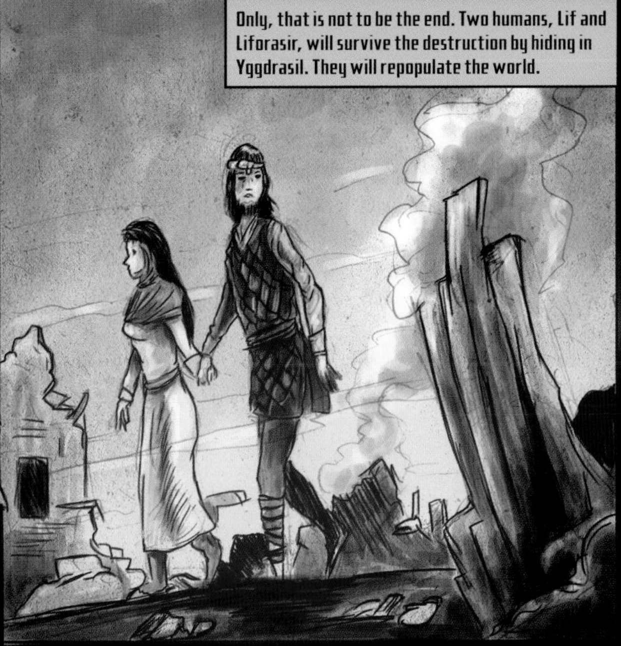
Only, that is not to be the end. Two humans, Lif and Lifarasir, will survive the destruction by hiding in Yggdrasil. They will repopulate the world.

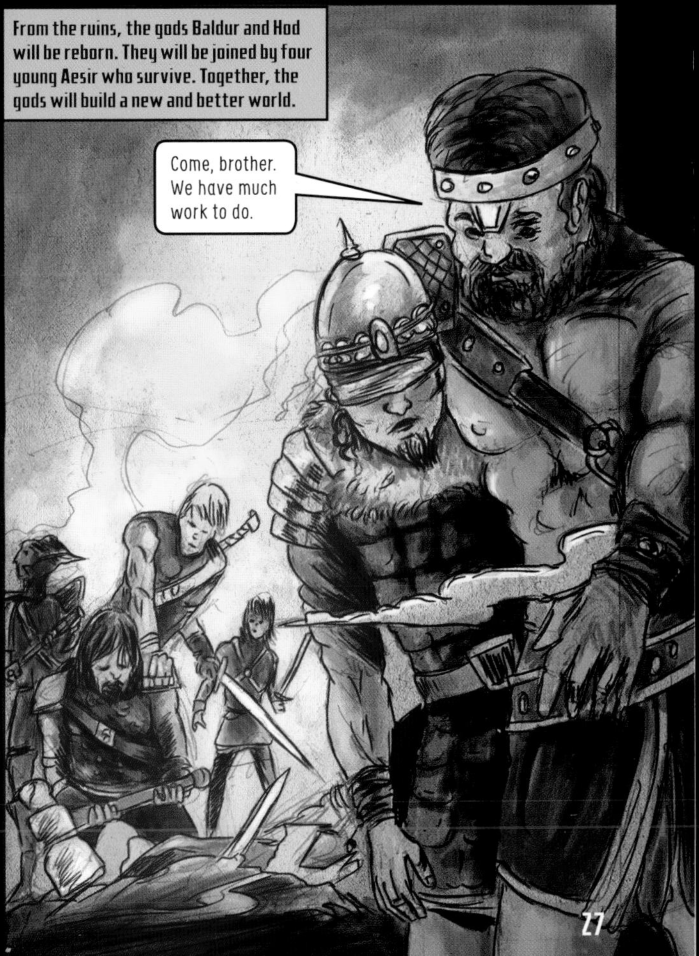
From the ruins, the gods Baldur and Hod will be reborn. They will be joined by four young Aesir who survive. Together, the gods will build a new and better world.
Come, brother. We have much work to do.

CHAPTER FIVE

THE FIVE SUNS

AN AZTEC MYTH

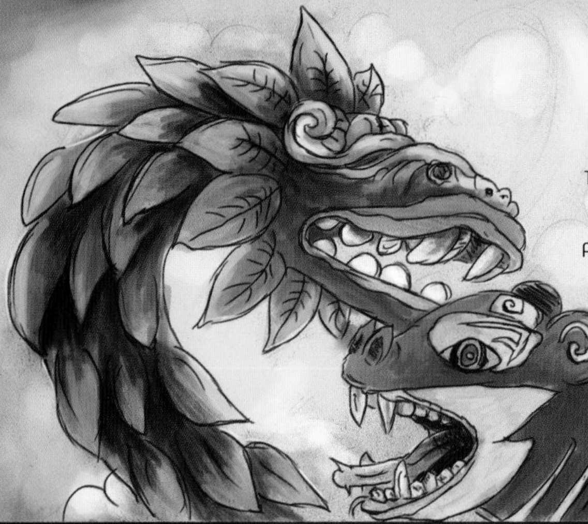

THE AZTECS BELIEVED OTHER WORLDS EXISTED BEFORE THIS ONE. THEY CALLED EACH WORLD A SUN. EVERY NEW SUN WAS FORMED FROM A GOD. BUT TWO JEALOUS GODS NAMED TEZCATLIPOCA (TEHS-KAH-TLEE-**POH**-KAH) AND QUETZALCOATL (KET-SAHL-**KOH**-AHTL) COULD NOT AGREE WHO SHOULD TAKE THE HONORED PLACE IN THE SKY. THEIR FIGHTING WOULD CAUSE TERRIBLE DESTRUCTION.

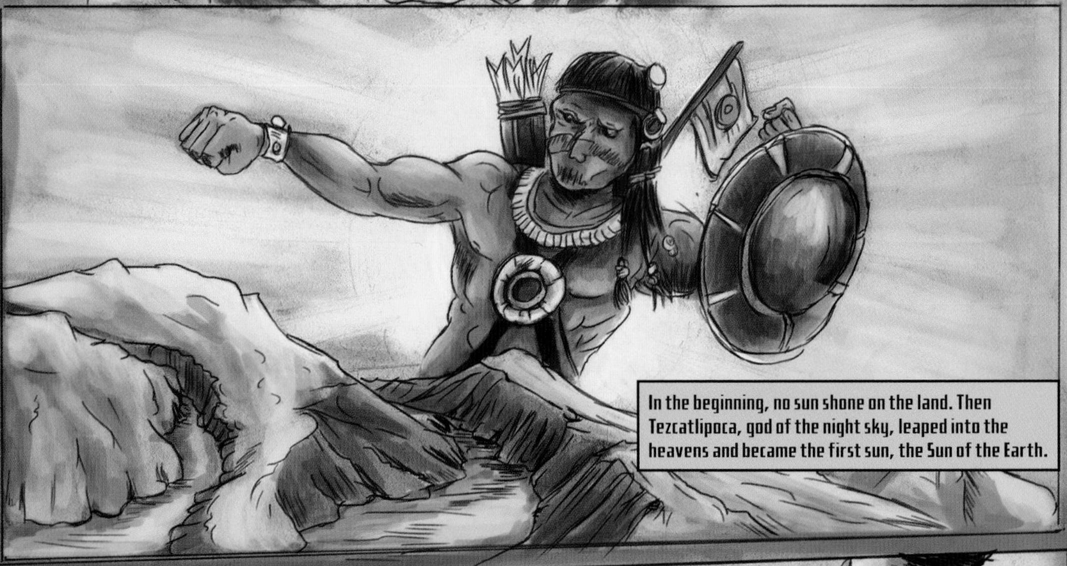
In the beginning, no sun shone on the land. Then Tezcatlipoca, god of the night sky, leaped into the heavens and became the first sun, the Sun of the Earth.

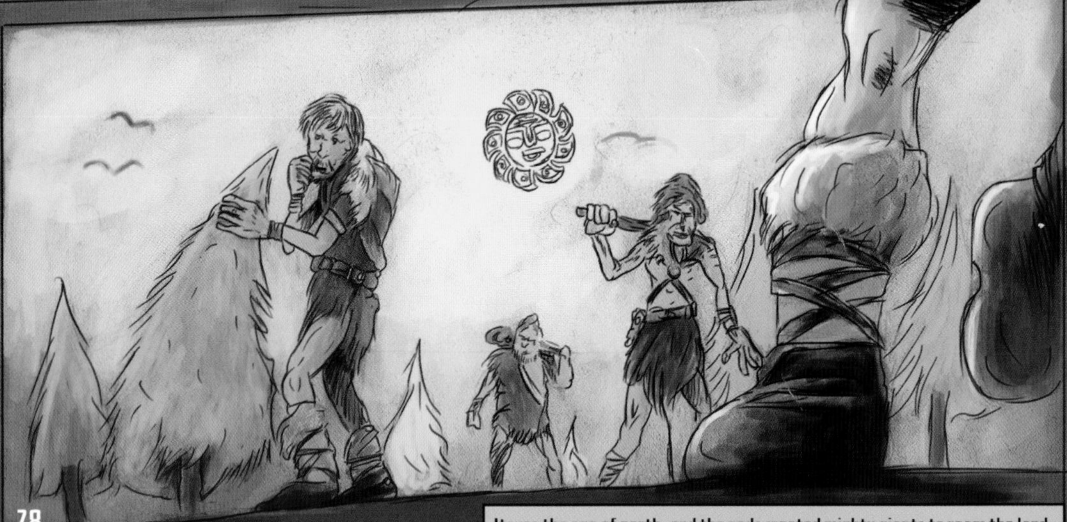
It was the age of earth, and the gods created mighty giants to roam the land.

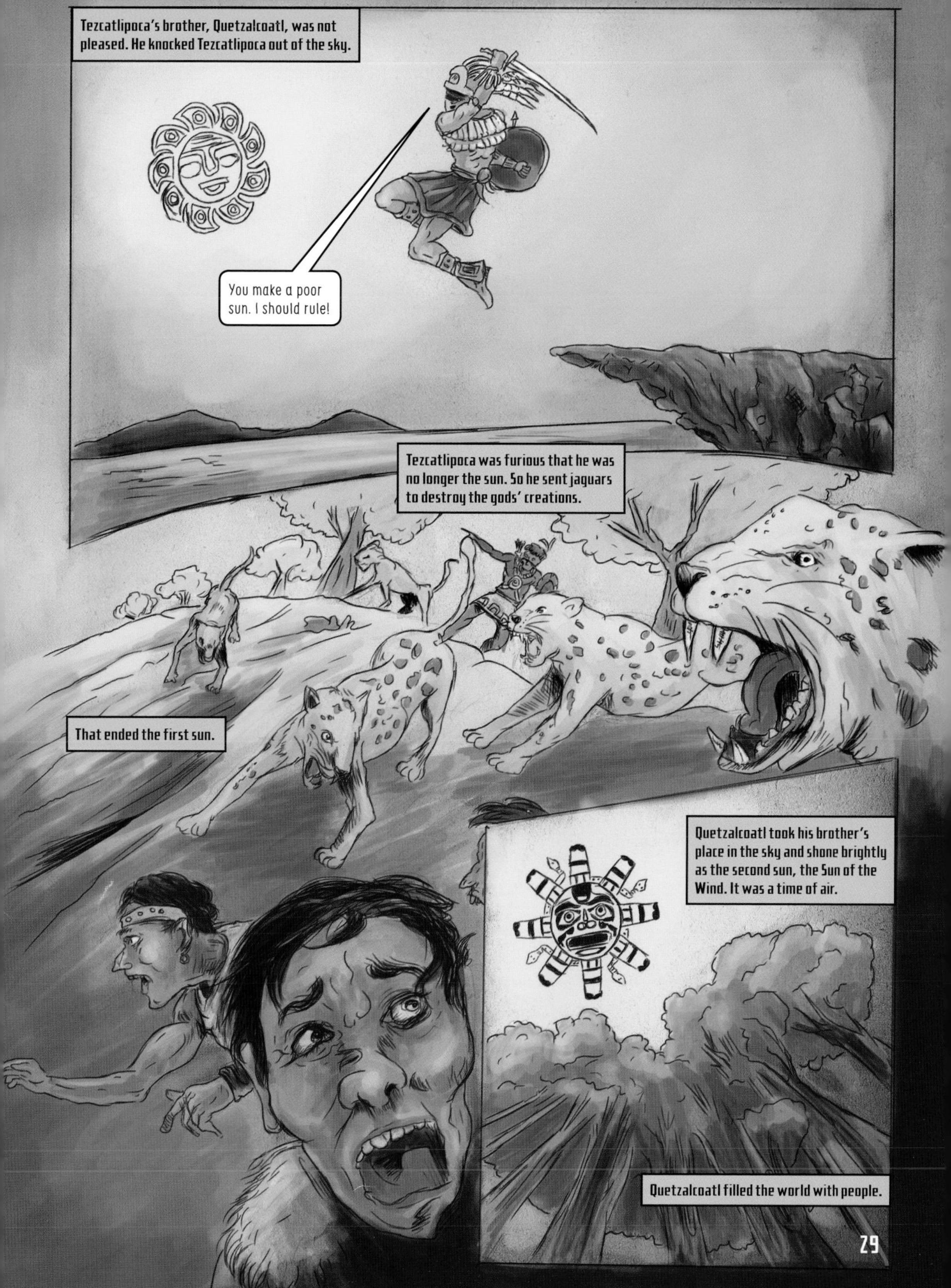

Tezcatlipoca's brother, Quetzalcoatl, was not pleased. He knocked Tezcatlipoca out of the sky.
You make a poor sun. I should rule!
Tezcatlipoca was furious that he was no longer the sun. So he sent jaguars to destroy the gods' creations.
That ended the first sun.
Quetzalcoatl took his brother's place in the sky and shone brightly as the second sun, the Sun of the Wind. It was a time of air.
Quetzalcoatl filled the world with people.

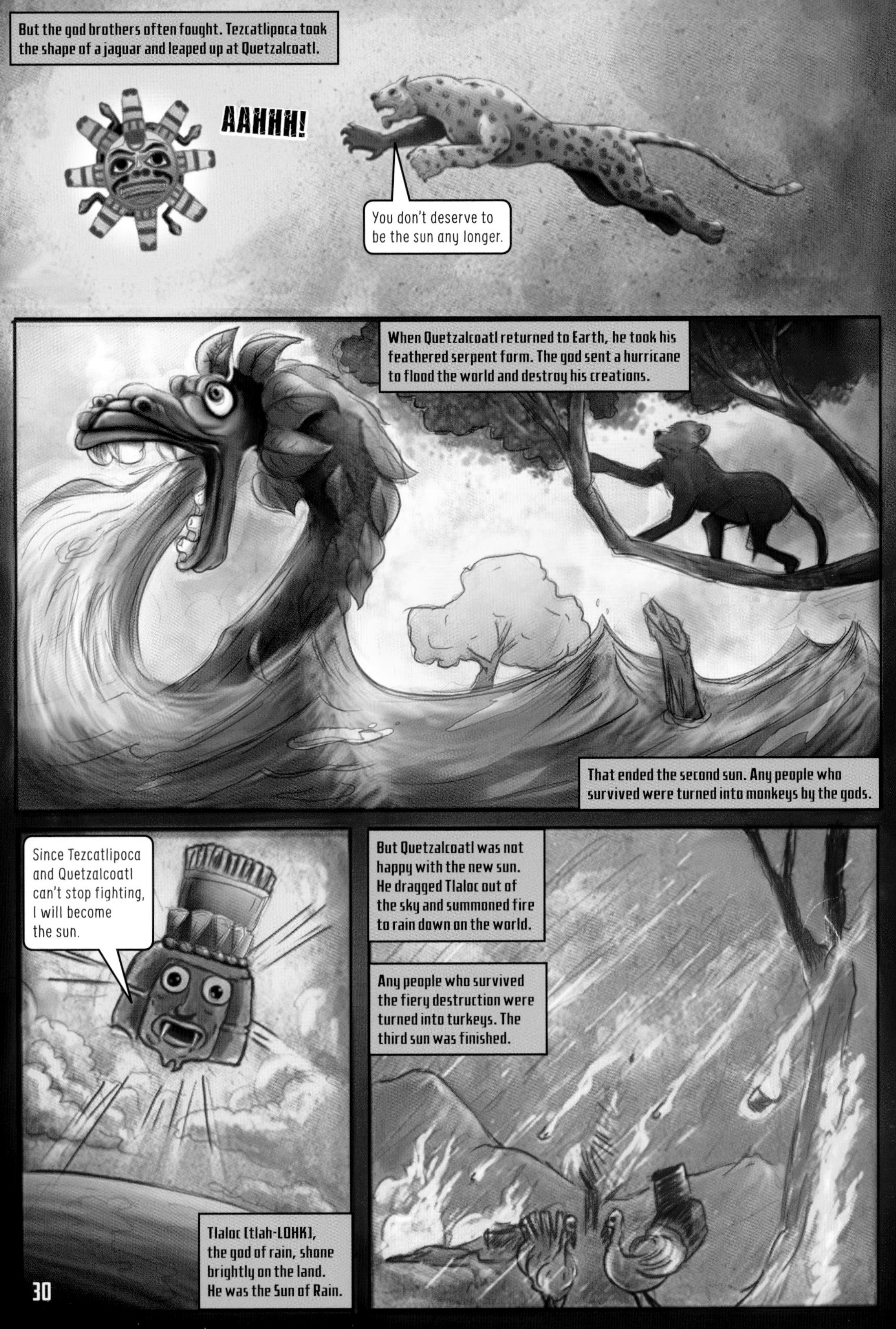

But the god brothers often fought. Tezcatlipoca took the shape of a jaguar and leaped up at Quetzalcoatl.
AAHHH!
You don't deserve to be the sun any longer.
When Quetzalcoatl returned to Earth, he took his feathered serpent form. The god sent a hurricane to flood the world and destroy his creations.
That ended the second sun. Any people who survived were turned into monkeys by the gods.
Since Tezcatlipoca and Quetzalcoatl can't stop fighting, I will become the sun.
Tlaloc [tlah-LOHK], the god of rain, shone brightly on the land. He was the Sun of Rain.
But Quetzalcoatl was not happy with the new sun. He dragged Tlaloc out of the sky and summoned fire to rain down on the world.
Any people who survived the fiery destruction were turned into turkeys. The third sun was finished.

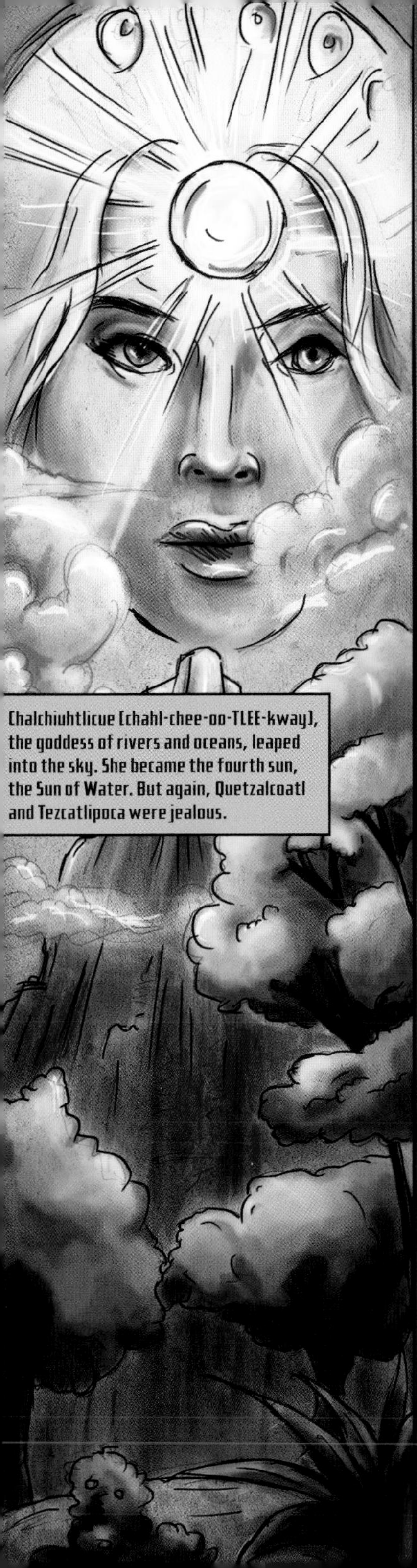
Chalchiuhtlicue [chahl-chee-oo-TLEE-kway], the goddess of rivers and oceans, leaped into the sky. She became the fourth sun, the Sun of Water. But again, Quetzalcoatl and Tezcatlipoca were jealous.

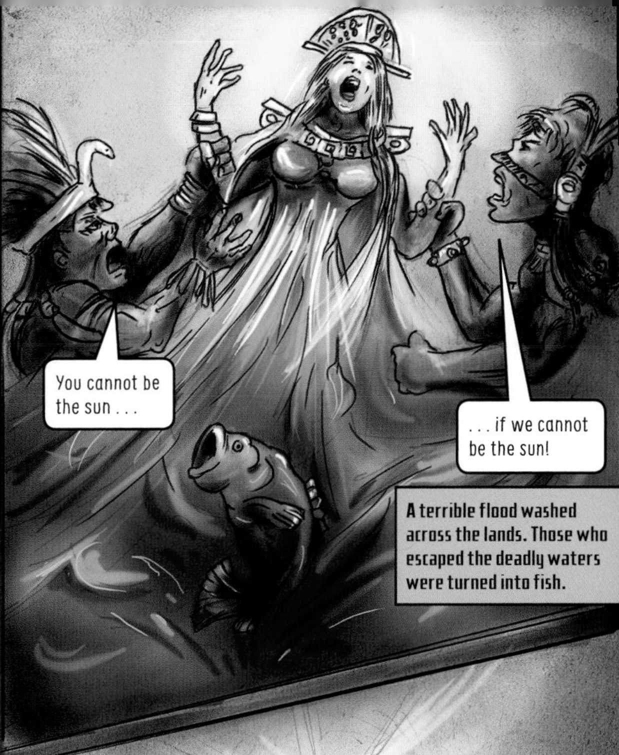
You cannot be the sun . . .
. . . if we cannot be the sun!
A terrible flood washed across the lands. Those who escaped the deadly waters were turned into fish.

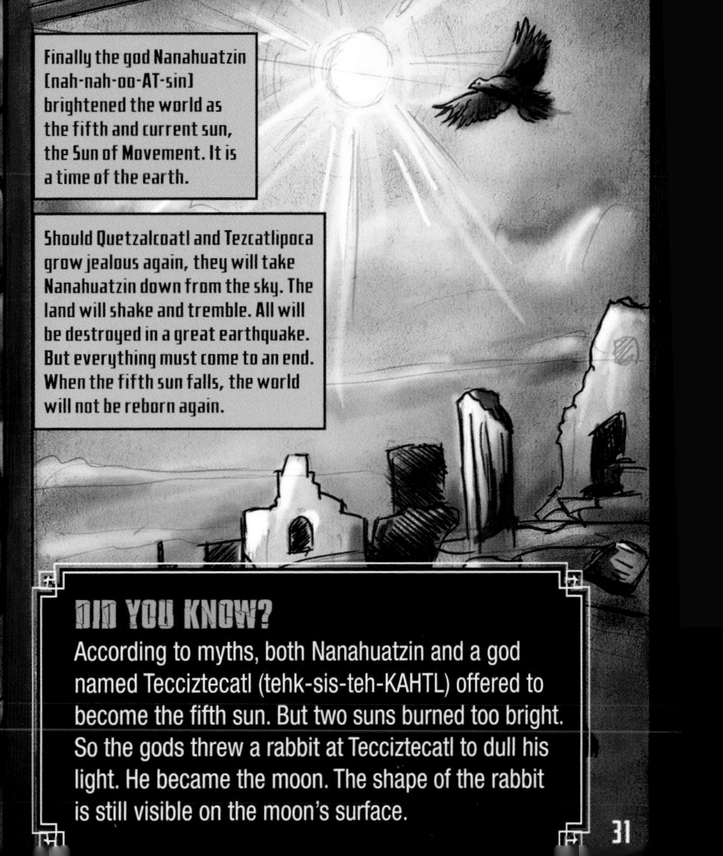
Finally the god Nanahuatzin [nah-nah-oo-AT-sin] brightened the world as the fifth and current sun, the Sun of Movement. It is a time of the earth.
Should Quetzalcoatl and Tezcatlipoca grow jealous again, they will take Nanahuatzin down from the sky. The land will shake and tremble. All will be destroyed in a great earthquake. But everything must come to an end. When the fifth sun falls, the world will not be reborn again.

DID YOU KNOW?

According to myths, both Nanahuatzin and a god named Tecciztecatl (tehk-sis-teh-KAHTL) offered to become the fifth sun. But two suns burned too bright. So the gods threw a rabbit at Tecciztecatl to dull his light. He became the moon. The shape of the rabbit is still visible on the moon's surface.

CHAPTER SIX

THE COSMIC SERPENT

A FON MYTH

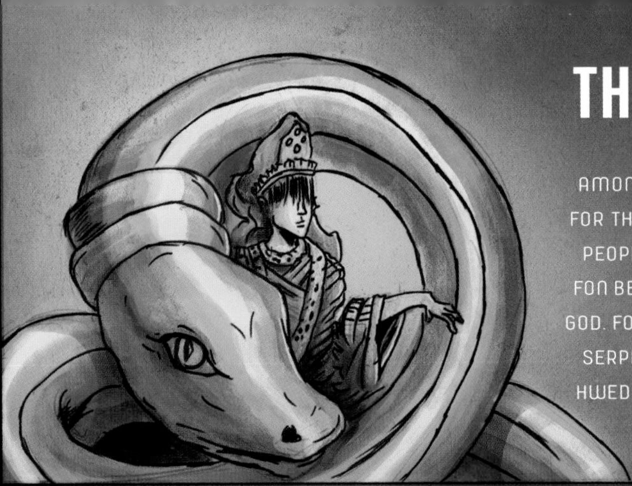

AMONG AFRICAN CULTURES, THE FON ARE KNOWN FOR THEIR COLORFUL MYTHS. THESE WEST AFRICAN PEOPLE LIVE MOSTLY IN BENIN AND NIGERIA. THE FON BELIEVED THAT NANA-BULUKU WAS THE FIRST GOD. FOR A COMPANION, SHE HAD A GIANT RAINBOW SERPENT CALLED AIDO-HWEDO. ALTHOUGH AIDO-HWEDO HELPED CREATE THE WORLD, THE SERPENT WILL ONE DAY BRING ABOUT ITS END.

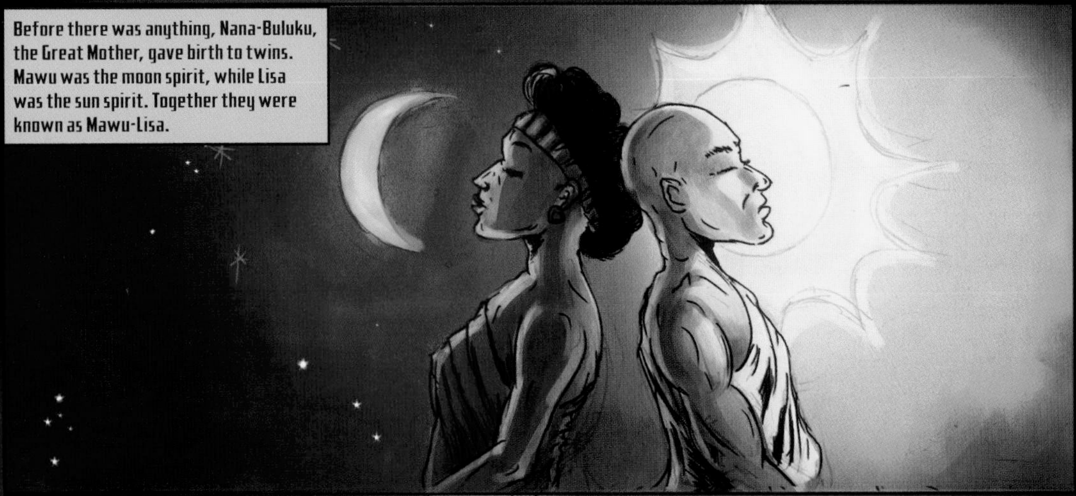
Before there was anything, Nana-Buluku, the Great Mother, gave birth to twins. Mawu was the moon spirit, while Lisa was the sun spirit. Together they were known as Mawu-Lisa.

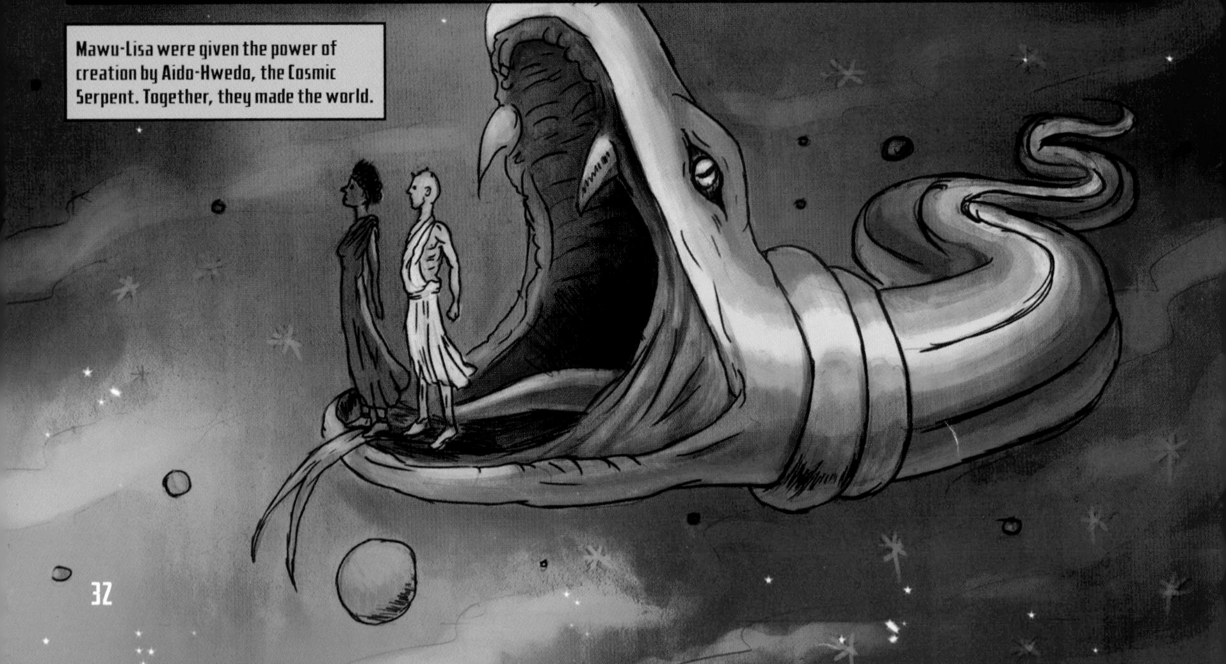
Mawu-Lisa were given the power of creation by Aido-Hwedo, the Cosmic Serpent. Together, they made the world.

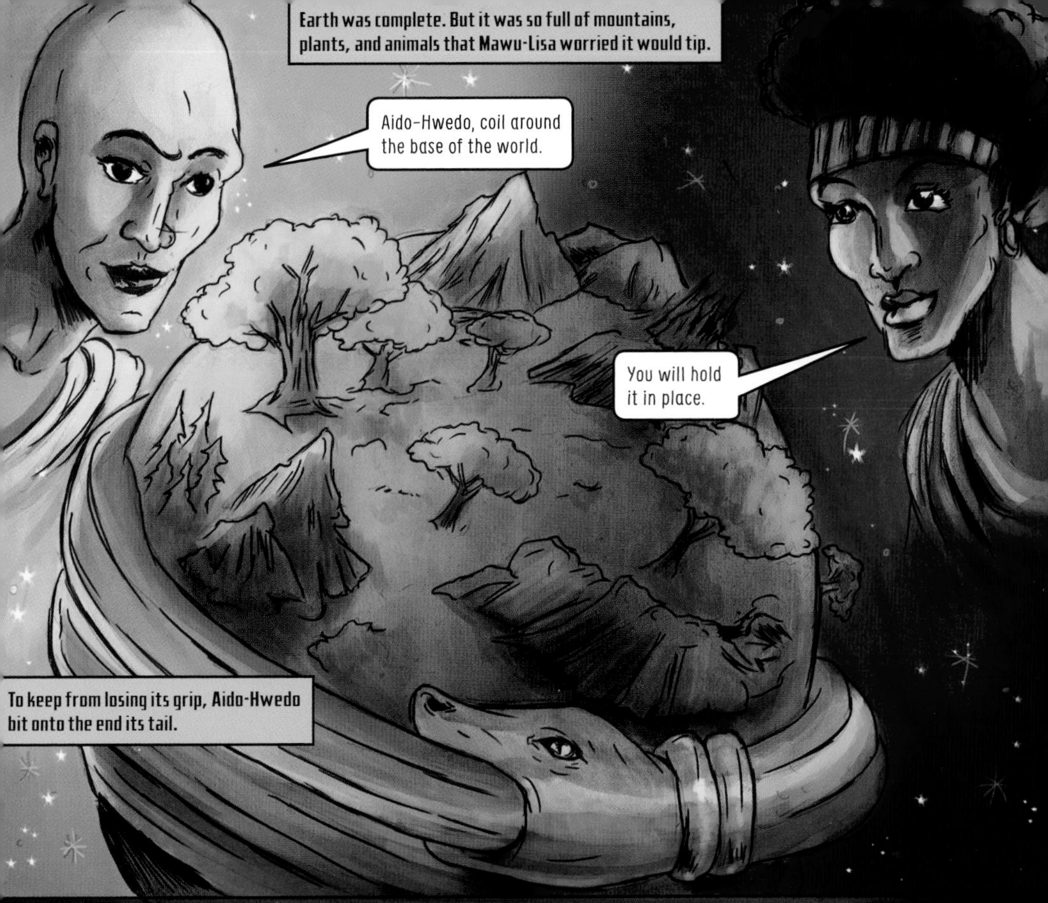
Earth was complete. But it was so full of mountains, plants, and animals that Mawu-Lisa worried it would tip.
Aido-Hwedo, coil around the base of the world.
You will hold it in place.
To keep from losing its grip, Aido-Hwedo bit onto the end its tail.

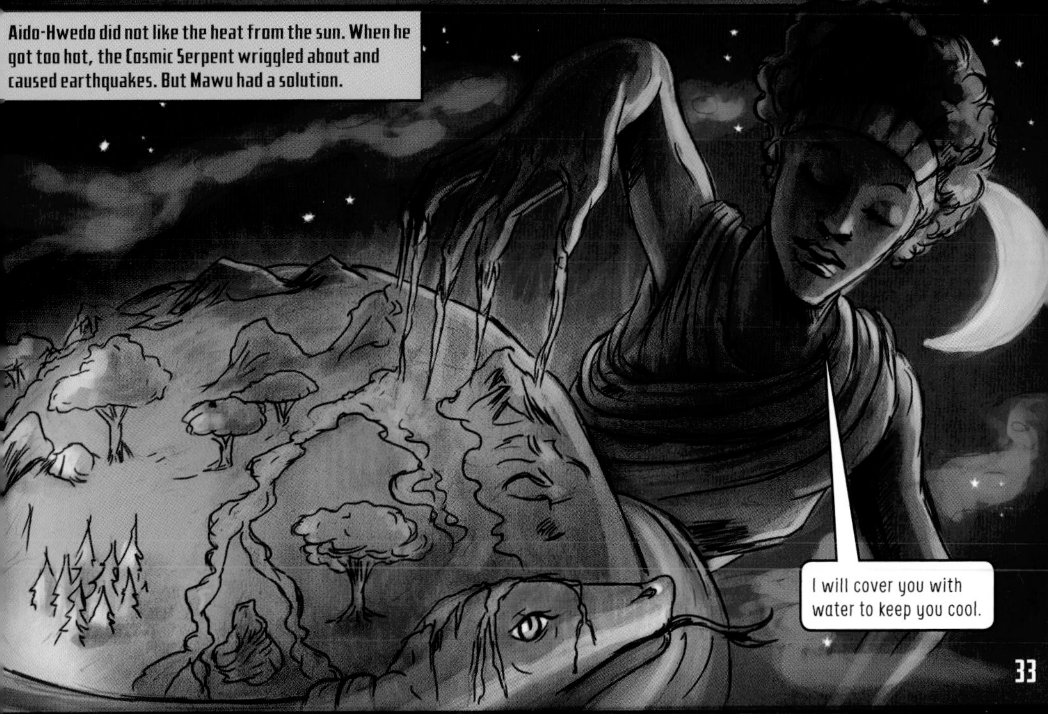
Aido-Hwedo did not like the heat from the sun. When he got too hot, the Cosmic Serpent wriggled about and caused earthquakes. But Mawu had a solution.
I will cover you with water to keep you cool.

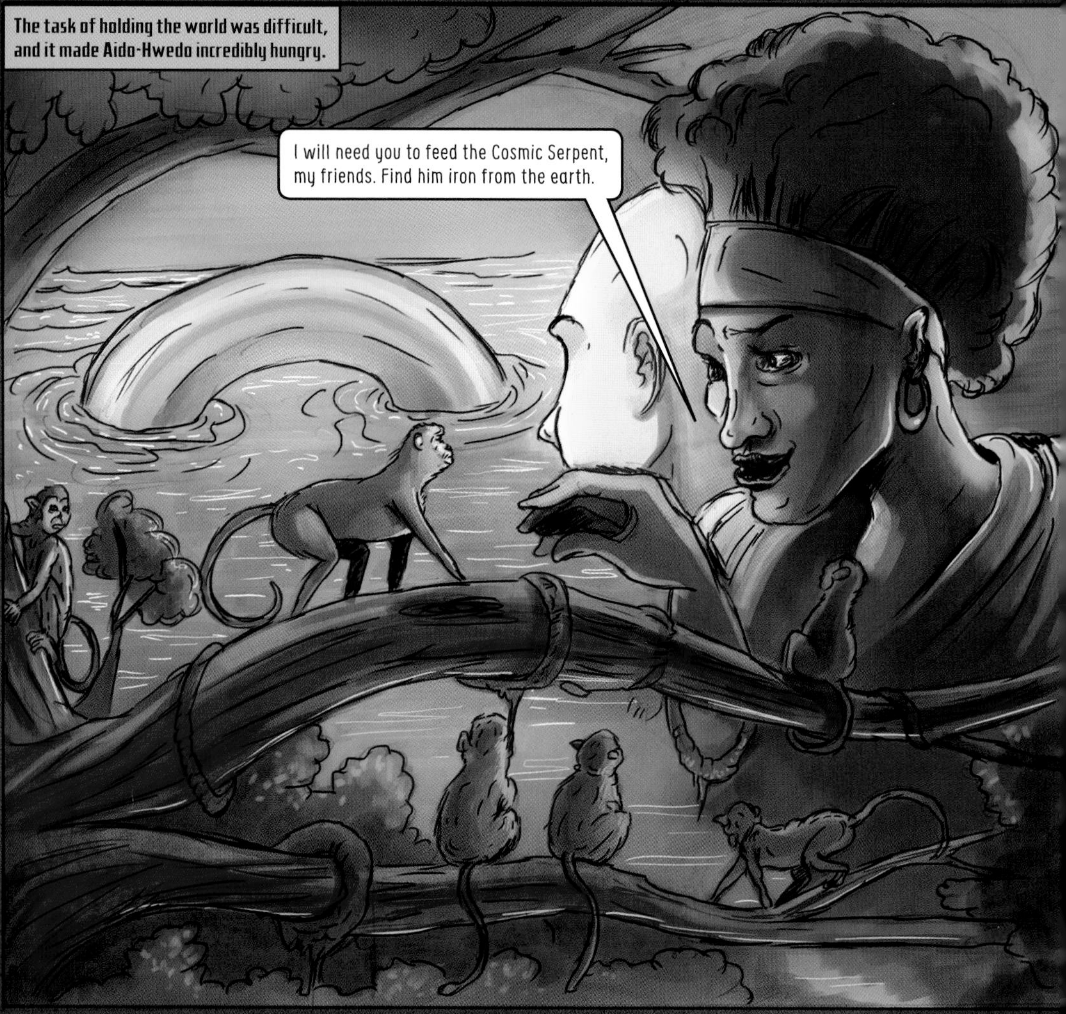
The task of holding the world was difficult, and it made Aido-Hwedo incredibly hungry.
I will need you to feed the Cosmic Serpent, my friends. Find him iron from the earth.

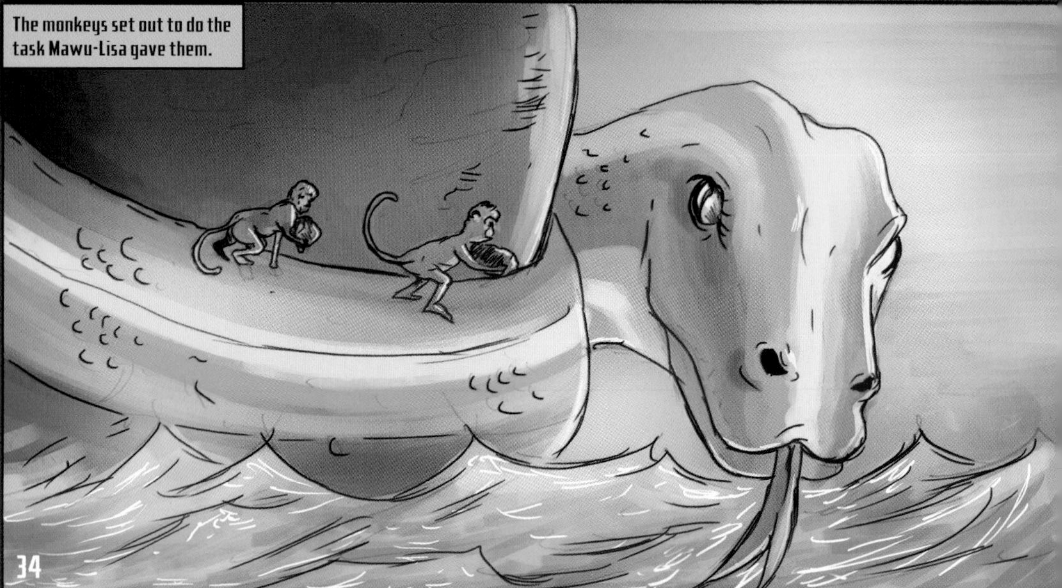
The monkeys set out to do the task Mawu-Lisa gave them.

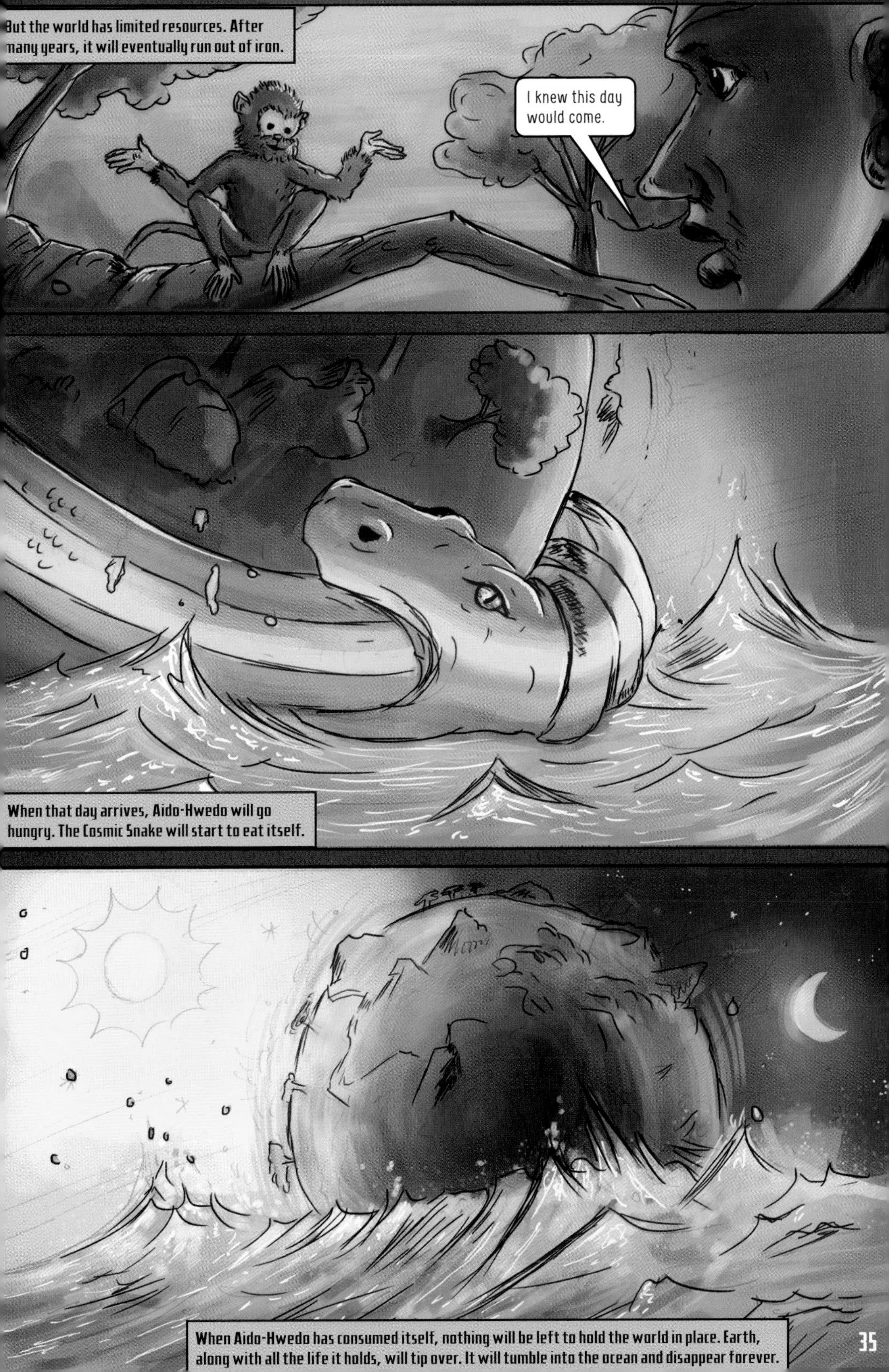
But the world has limited resources. After many years, it will eventually run out of iron.
I knew this day would come.
When that day arrives, Aido-Hwedo will go hungry. The Cosmic Snake will start to eat itself.
When Aido-Hwedo has consumed itself, nothing will be left to hold the world in place. Earth, along with all the life it holds, will tip over. It will tumble into the ocean and disappear forever.

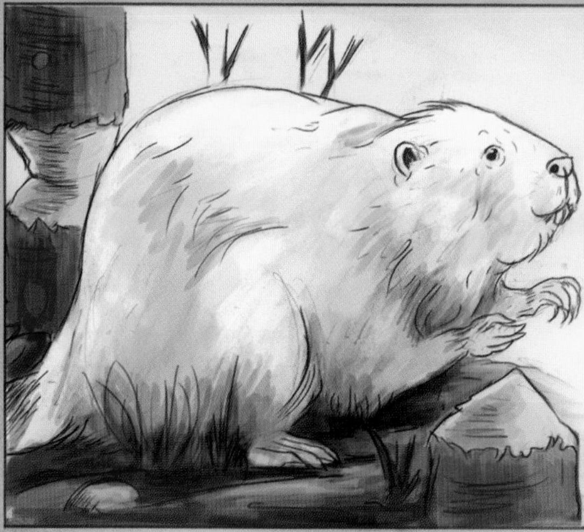

CHAPTER SEVEN

GREAT WHITE GRANDFATHER BEAVER

A CHEYENNE MYTH

IN NATIVE AMERICAN LEGENDS, ANIMAL SPIRITS PLAY IMPORTANT ROLES. COYOTE IS OFTEN A TRICKSTER WHO GETS INTO TROUBLE. IN SOME TALES, TURTLE CARRIES THE WORLD UPON HIS BACK. TO THE CHEYENNE PEOPLE FROM THE GREAT PLAINS, THE GREAT WHITE GRANDFATHER BEAVER OF THE NORTH WILL EVENTUALLY BRING LIFE TO AN END.

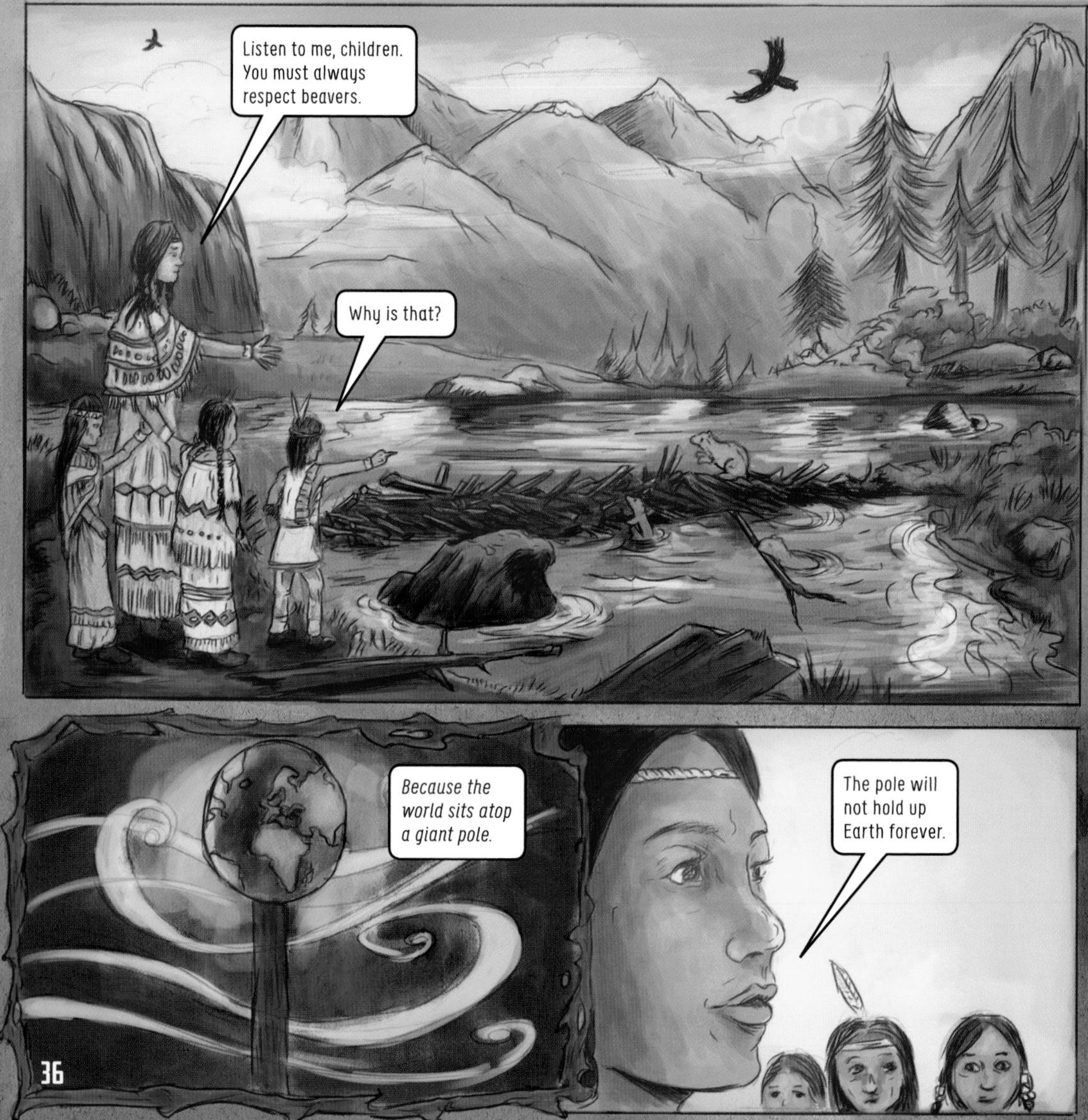
Listen to me, children. You must always respect beavers.
Why is that?
Because the world sits atop a giant pole.
The pole will not hold up Earth forever.

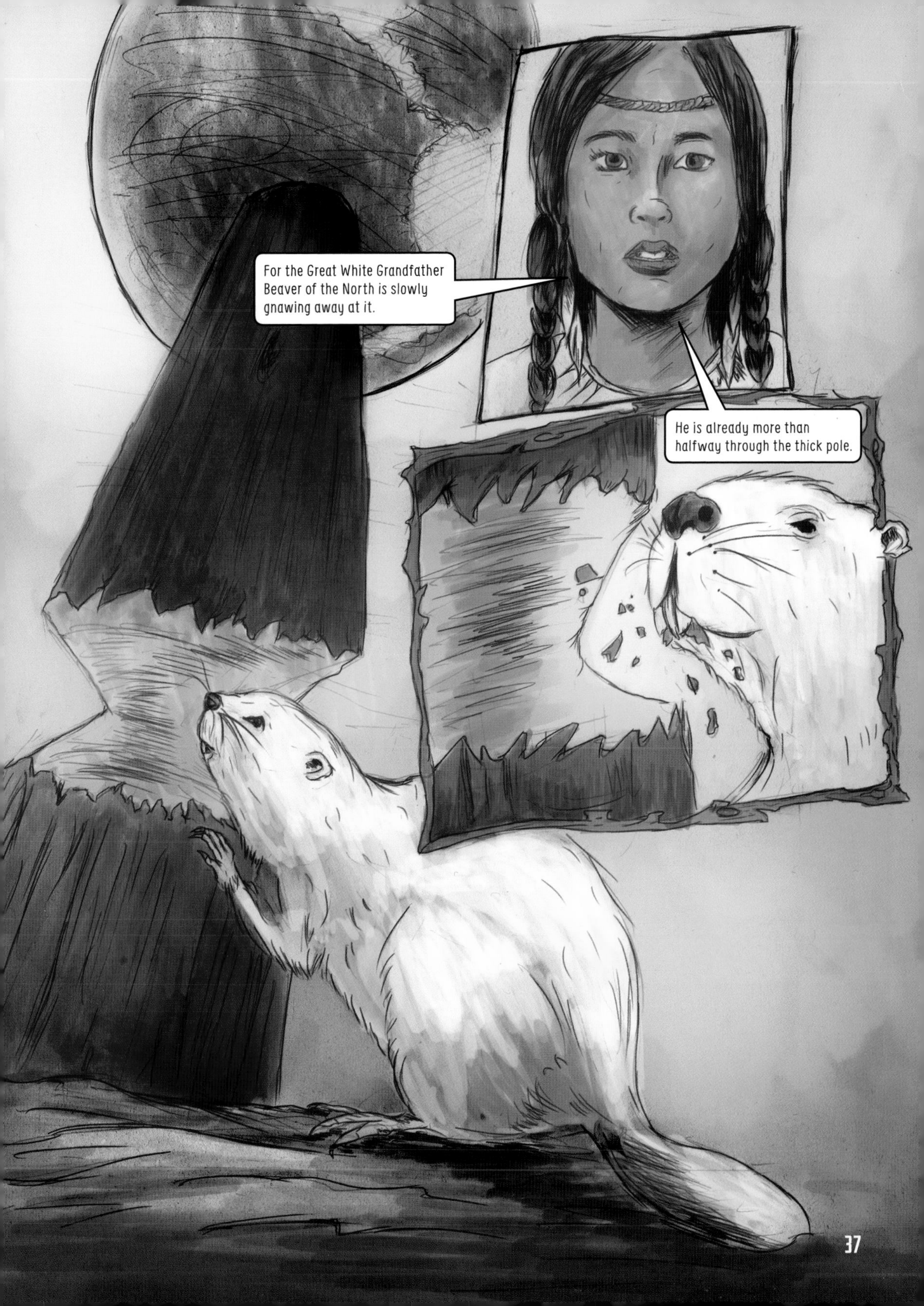
For the Great White Grandfather Beaver of the North is slowly gnawing away at it.
He is already more than halfway through the thick pole.

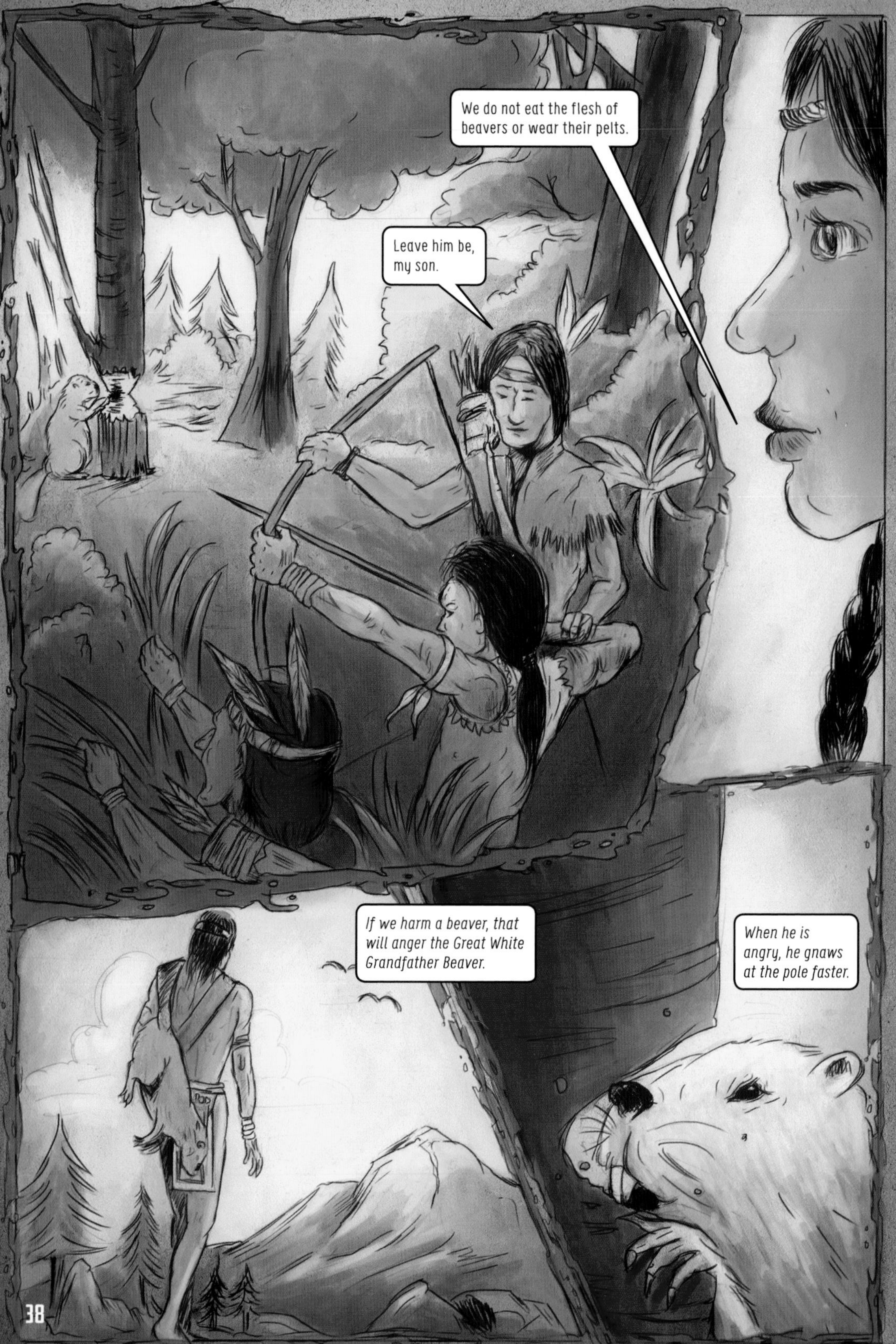
We do not eat the flesh of beavers or wear their pelts.
Leave him be, my son.
If we harm a beaver, that will anger the Great White Grandfather Beaver.
When he is angry, he gnaws at the pole faster.

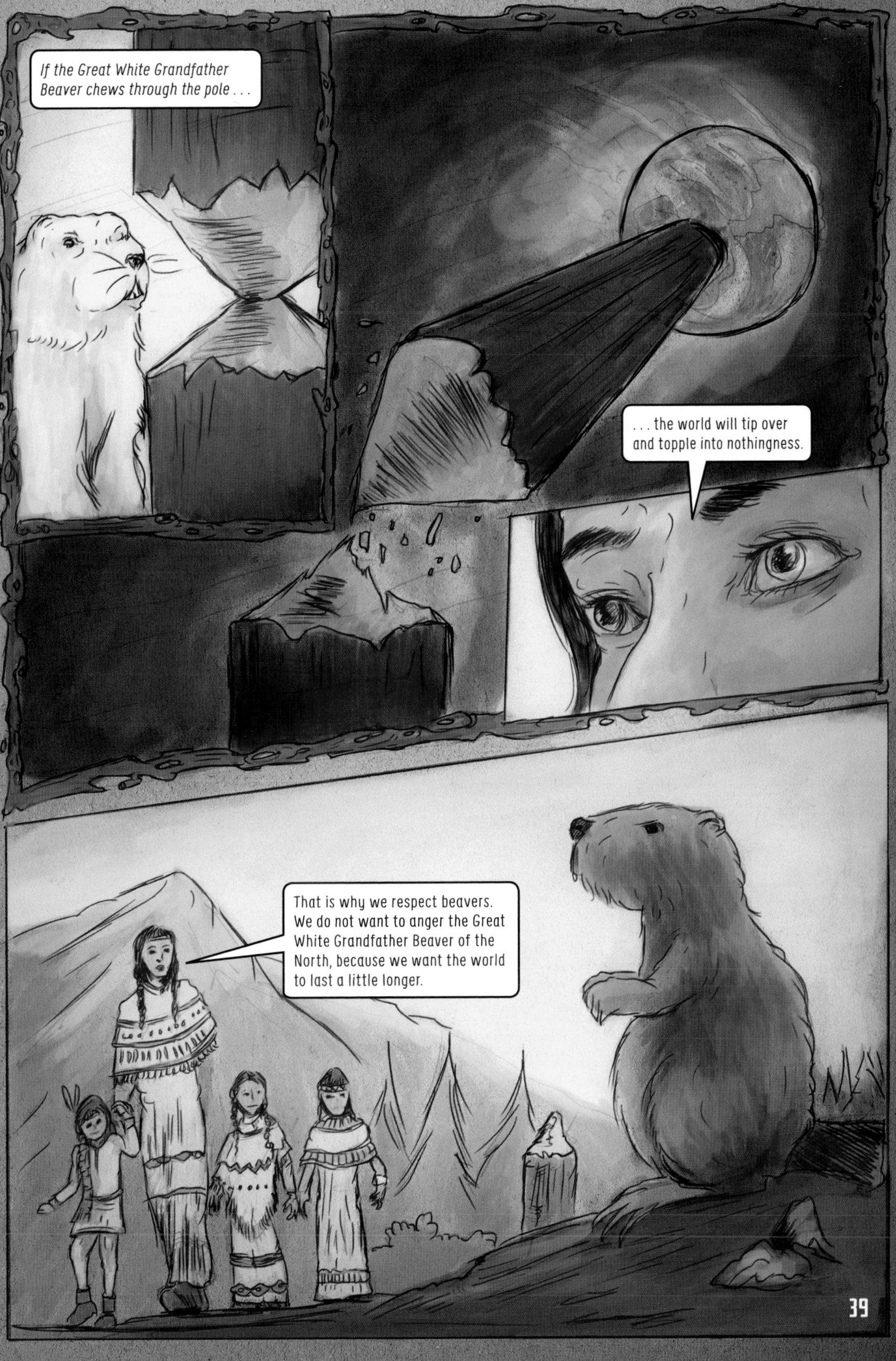
If the Great White Grandfather Beaver chews through the pole . . .
. . . the world will tip over and topple into nothingness.
That is why we respect beavers. We do not want to anger the Great White Grandfather Beaver of the North, because we want the world to last a little longer.

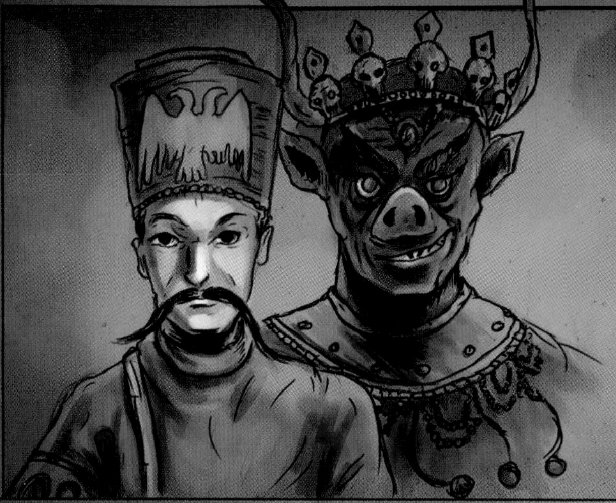

CHAPTER EIGHT

RULER OF THE UNDERWORLD

A MONGOLIAN MYTH

BY THE 1400S, THE MONGOLIAN EMPIRE HAD GROWN INTO THE LARGEST EMPIRE TO EVER EXIST. WITHIN THE EMPIRE WERE MANY DIFFERENT CULTURES AND MANY MYTHS. IN ONE STORY, THE GOD ULGEN CREATES ERLIK, THE FIRST MAN. BUT ULGEN DID NOT KNOW THAT HIS OWN CREATION WOULD ONE DAY RISE AGAINST HIM.

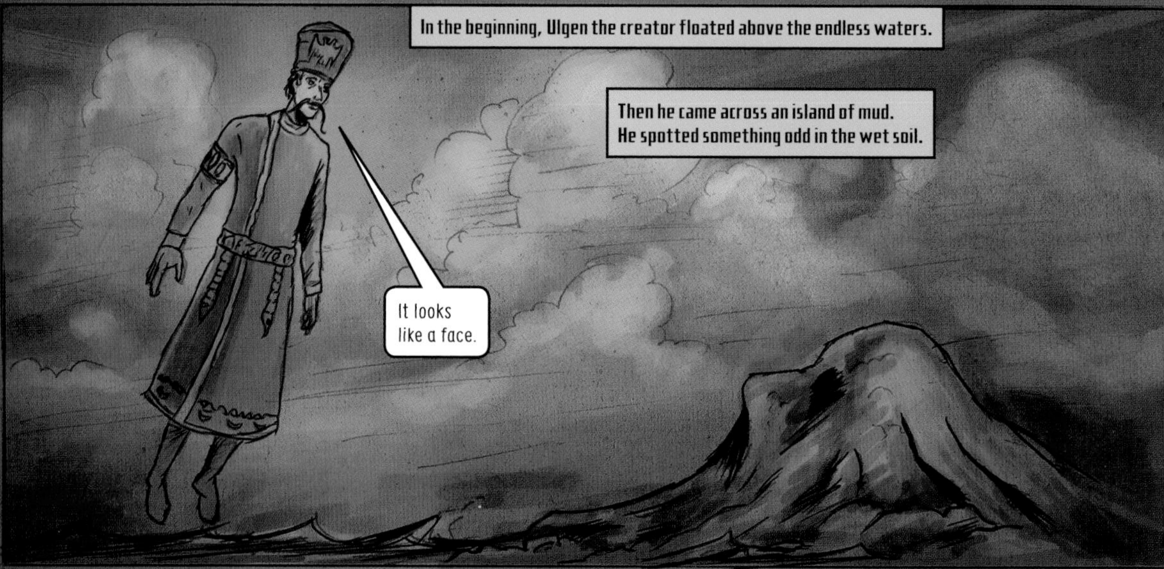
In the beginning, Ulgen the creator floated above the endless waters.
Then he came across an island of mud. He spotted something odd in the wet soil.
It looks like a face.

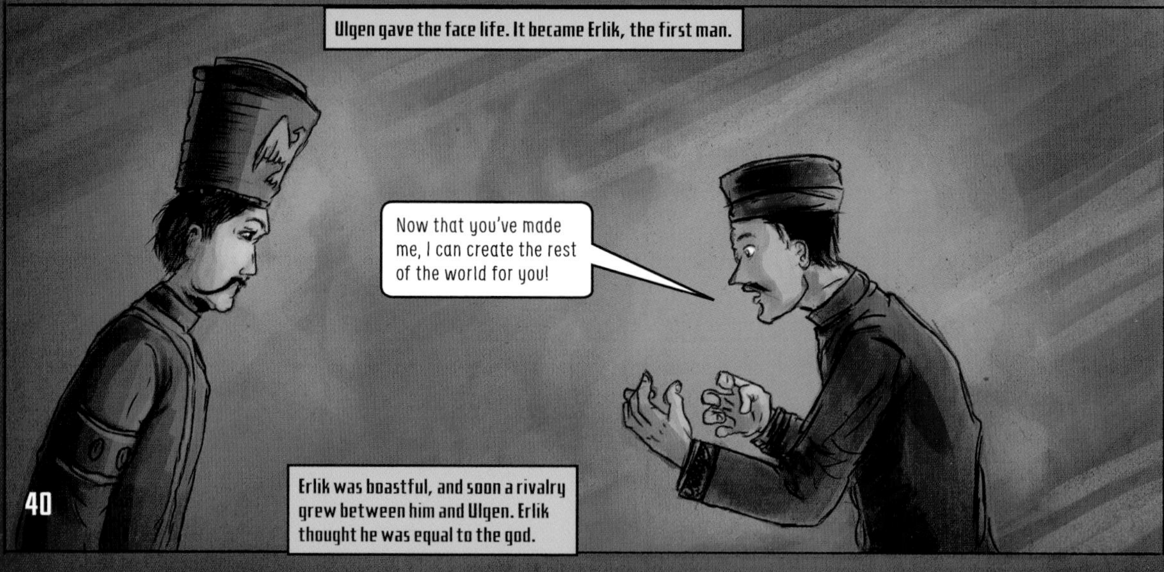
Ulgen gave the face life. It became Erlik, the first man.
Now that you've made me, I can create the rest of the world for you!
Erlik was boastful, and soon a rivalry grew between him and Ulgen. Erlik thought he was equal to the god.

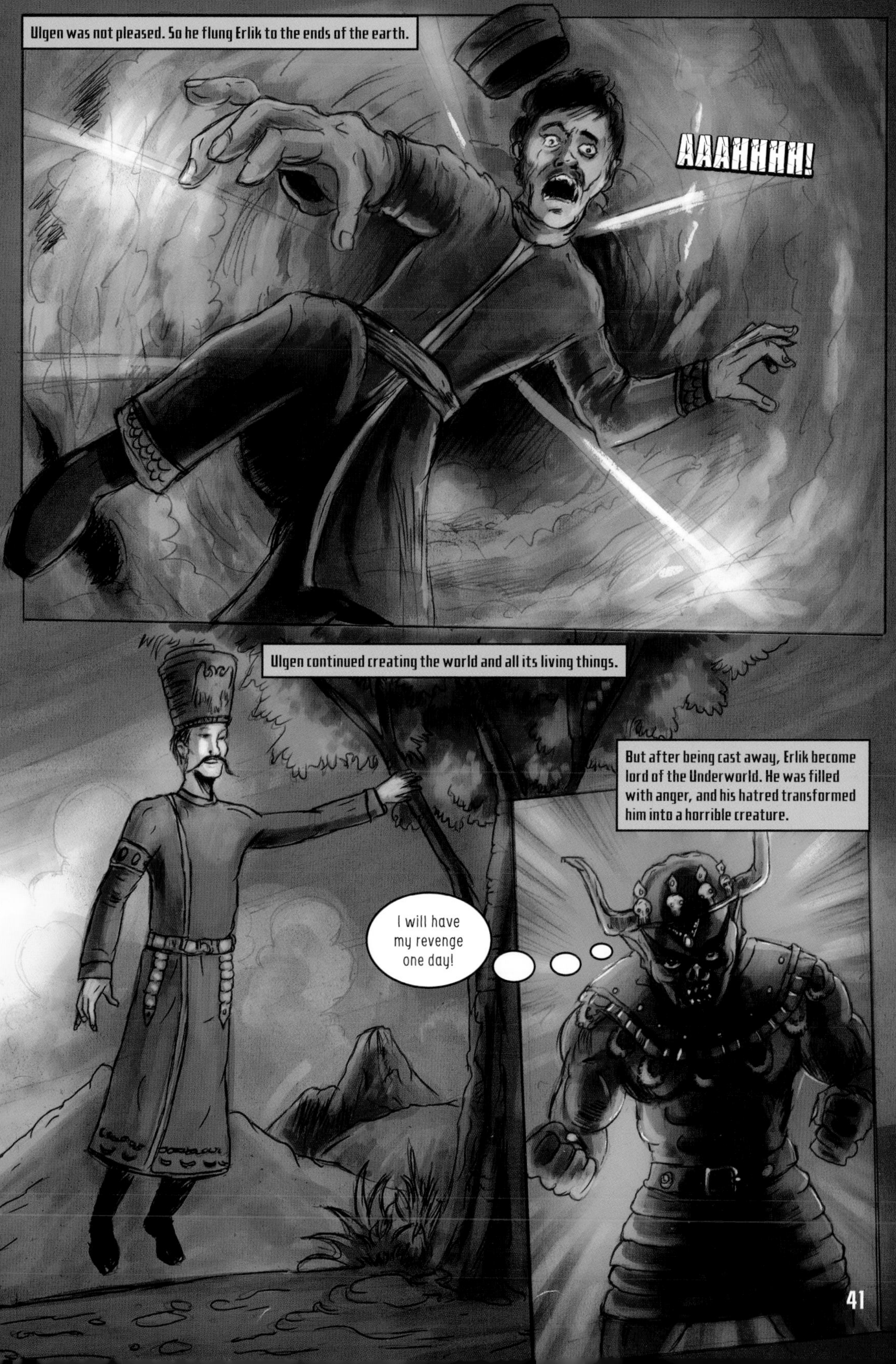
Ulgen was not pleased. So he flung Erlik to the ends of the earth.
AAAHHHH!
Ulgen continued creating the world and all its living things.
But after being cast away, Erlik become lord of the Underworld. He was filled with anger, and his hatred transformed him into a horrible creature.
I will have my revenge one day!

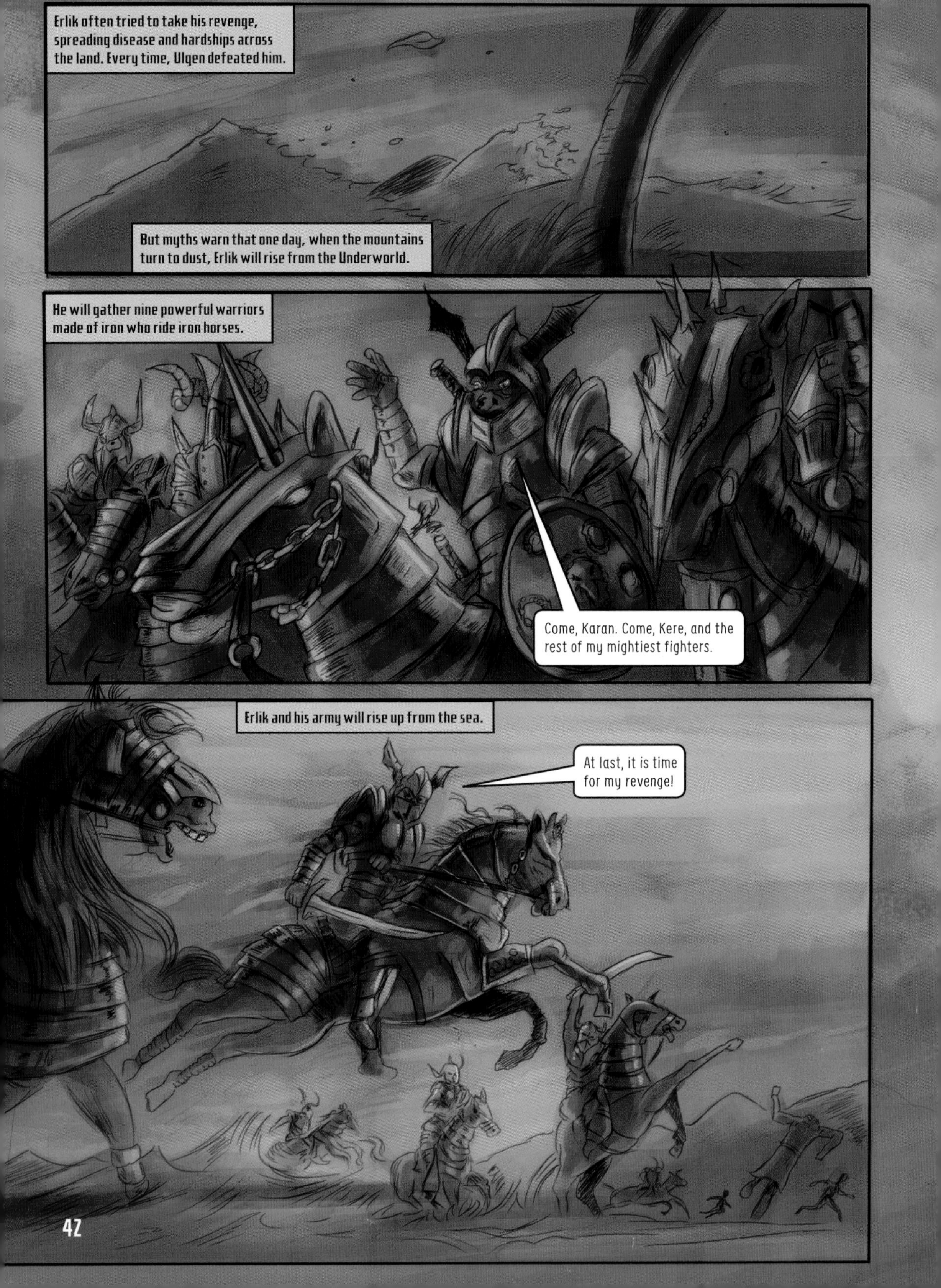
Erlik often tried to take his revenge, spreading disease and hardships across the land. Every time, Ulgen defeated him.
But myths warn that one day, when the mountains turn to dust, Erlik will rise from the Underworld.
He will gather nine powerful warriors made of iron who ride iron horses.
Come, Karan. Come, Kere, and the rest of my mightiest fighters.
Erlik and his army will rise up from the sea.
At last, it is time for my revenge!

READ MORE

Chambers, Catherine. *American Indian Stories and Legends.* All About Myths. Chicago: Raintree, 2014.

Hoena, Blake. *Everything Mythology.* National Geographic Kids Everything. Washington, DC: National Geographic Children's Books, 2014.

Krieg, Katherine. *What We Get from Greek Mythology.* Mythology and Culture. Ann Arbor, Mich.: Cherry Lake Publishing, 2015.

Roxburgh, Ellis. *The Mesopotamian Empires.* Great Empires. New York: Cavendish Square Publishing, 2016.

CRITICAL THINKING QUESTIONS

1. The myths in this book show various ways in which the world could end. Sometimes everything gets washed away in a flood. In other myths, the world gets destroyed in fire or wiped out in a bloody battle between the gods. Imagine another way in which the world could end. Then write your own myth.

2. The ancient Greeks believed there were other ages of men before them. The first people were considered superior. But in each new age, people were considered inferior to those who came before. Why do you think the Greeks came to believe in such stories?

3. Although the myths retold here are from different cultures, they often share similarities. Pick two myths. Using specific examples from the stories, write down the ways they are similar and how they are different.

INTERNET SITES

Use FactHound to find Internet sites related to this book.

Visit *www.facthound.com*

Just type in 9781515766261 and go!

 **Super-cool stuff!** Check out projects, games and lots more at **www.capstonekids.com**

INDEX

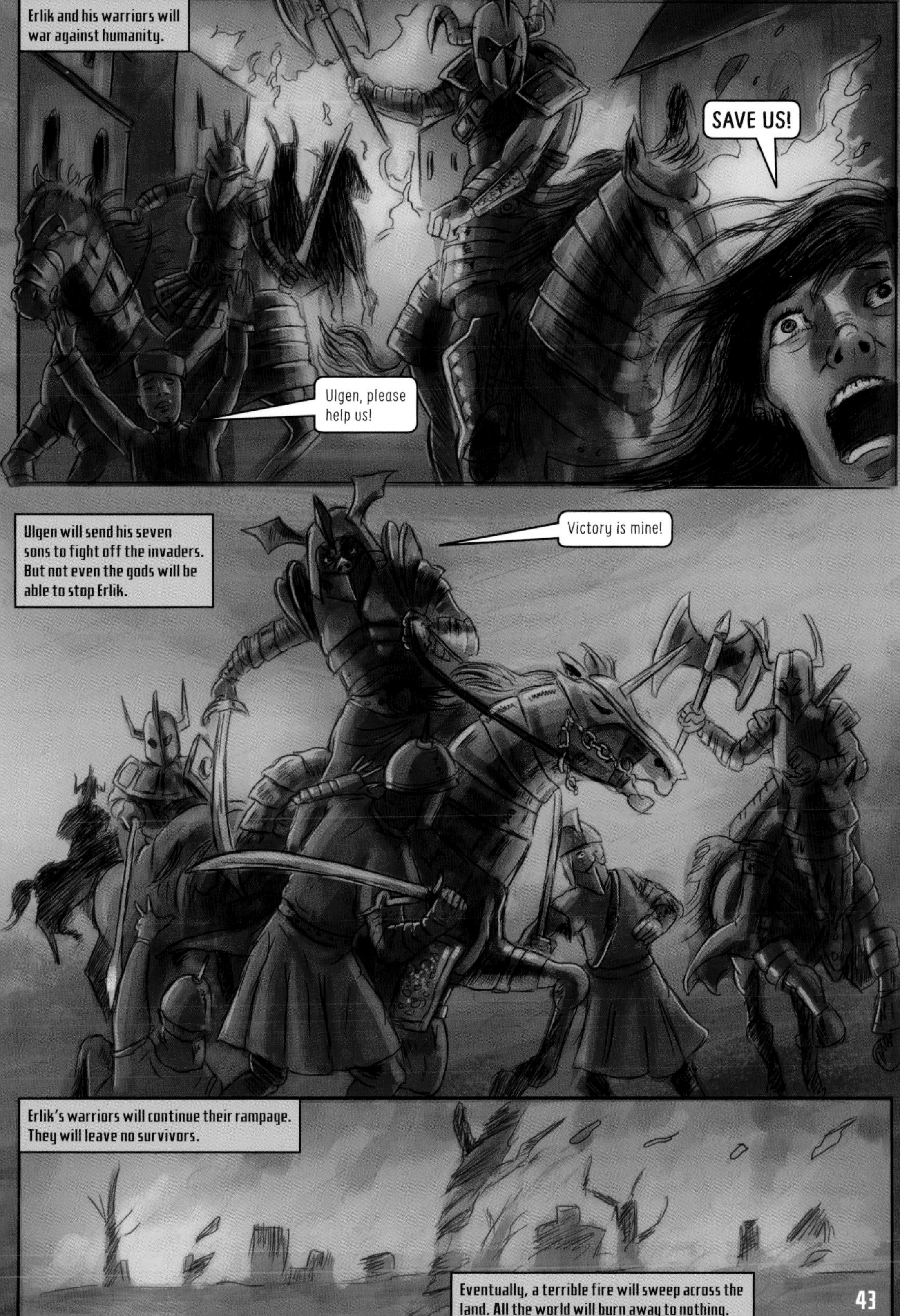
Erlik and his warriors will war against humanity.
SAVE US!
Ulgen, please help us!
Ulgen will send his seven sons to fight off the invaders. But not even the gods will be able to stop Erlik.
Victory is mine!
Erlik's warriors will continue their rampage. They will leave no survivors.
Eventually, a terrible fire will sweep across the land. All the world will burn away to nothing.

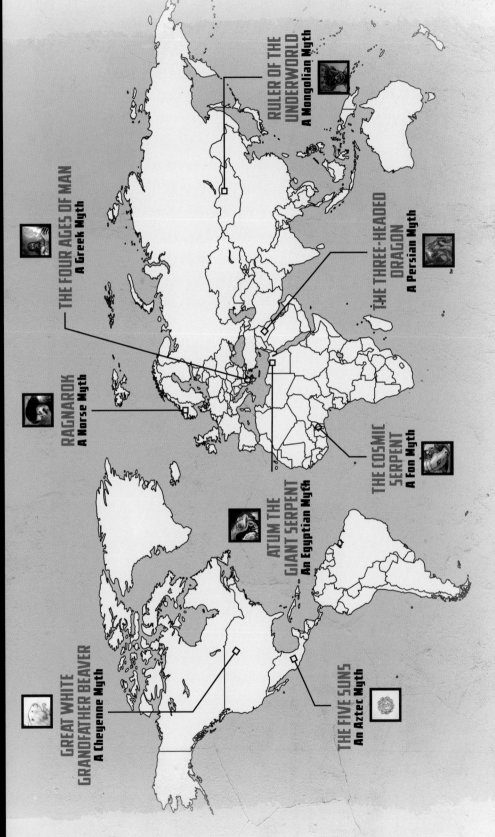

MYTH MAP AND MORE

RULER OF THE UNDERWORLD
A Mongolian Myth

THE FOUR AGES OF MAN
A Greek Myth

THE THREE-HEADED DRAGON
A Persian Myth

RAGNAROK
A Norse Myth

THE COSMIC SERPENT
A Fon Myth

ATUM THE GIANT SERPENT
An Egyptian Myth

GREAT WHITE GRANDFATHER BEAVER
A Cheyenne Myth

THE FIVE SUNS
An Aztec Myth

- The word *myth* comes from the Greek word *mythos*, which means "story." *Mythology* can refer to the study of myths, to a single collection of myths, or to all myths from a group of people.

- More than four thousand years ago, the Assyrians ruled Mesopotamia, the land between the Tigris and Euphrates Rivers. An Assyrian stone tablet is believed to contain the oldest known prophecy telling of the end of the world. The tablet claims that Earth was breaking down because people were corrupt and that the world would soon end in destruction..

- Ovid was a Roman poet born in 43 BC. He wrote about the four ages of man in *Metamorphoses*. This collection of poems included some of the best-known Greek and Roman myths. Hesiod, who lived in the 700s BC, wrote about five ages of man in *Works and Days*.

- The Egyptian *Book of the Dead* is an ancient collection of spells said to help the spirits of the dead find their way to the afterlife. This book also contains the story of Atum telling Osiris how he will eventually end all existence.

- Most knowledge of Norse myths comes from the ancient text *Poetic Edda*. It is a collection of 34 Icelandic poems. Storytellers had recited these poems for many generations until they were finally written down in the late 1200s. No one knows exactly how old the stories are, but they are believed to have begun hundreds of years before they were recorded.

- The Fon from West Africa have what is known as an oral tradition. This means that many of their myths and history are not written down. Instead, the stories are told and passed from generation to generation.

GLOSSARY

age (EYJ)—a long period of time beginning and ending with specific events

chaos (KAY-os)—state of confusion and disorder

deities (DEE-i-teez)—godlike beings

era (ER-uh)—a long period of time associated with specific events

invulnerable (in-VUHL-ner-uh-buhl)—not capable of being injured

legend (LEJ-uhnd)—a story that is believed to be true but cannot be proven

myth (MYTH)—a story told by people in ancient times; myths often tried to explain natural events

oracle (OR-uh-kuhl)—a person whom a god speaks through; in myths, gods used oracles to predict the future or to tell people how to solve problems

primordial (prahy-MAWR-dee-uhl)—what came first

prophecy (PROF-uh-see)—a foretelling of the future

revenge (rih-VENJ)—an action taken in return for an injury or offense